Tree Spirits

Tales and Encounters

Tree Spirits

Tales and Encounters

written and illustrated by

Heather Preston

Sweet Olive Press

San Anselmo, California

The Green Man uttering leaves

Contents

And this our life

exempt from public haunt,

Finds tongues in trees,

books in the running brooks,

Sermons in stones,

and good in every thing.

William Shakespeare

The Winding Path

Bali

It all started at a New Year's party in Sausalito, California many years ago. A small group of traveling Balinese gamelan musicians had been engaged to play their exotic gongs, drums, and bells for the guests. It was perfectly enchanting; I wanted to talk with them so when they took a break I asked, through their interpreter, the question, "What do you find most different here from your country?" They talked among themselves for some time then the interpreter, obviously embarrassed, answered with a question of their own: "We wonder, where are your tree spirits?"

I was speechless. Tree spirits? They actually believed there were such beings? And they had them? But we didn't? If only I had I known then what I do now, there would certainly have been a few choice follow-up questions. Alas, I was ignorant.

And so it was that the question: "Where are your tree spirits?" started my journey of discovery and, in course of time, my pilgrimage to the magical island of Bali. My mission was to find somebody who could tell me firsthand about tree spirits, not the fairy tale ones but the real ones that the musicians knew. It soon became apparent once I was in Bali, however, that the Balinese are protective of such knowledge and don't easily share it with scoffing Westerners. Why had the musicians even asked such a question those years ago in California? Must have come at an unguarded moment.

I had only ten short days in Bali. Three days left and no leads. What to do? At that point, I remember standing at the crossroads in Ubud, hand on hip, imploring the Powers of the Universe or Whoever might be in charge

of connections that week to take over the search. Then I simply trusted that something would turn up. I really did, much to the relief of Alan, my long-suffering husband, glad to be on to other pursuits.

We hired a cab to explore the island, a common practice since nobody in his right mind drives in Bali. Agung-the-fearless was our driver, a gregarious, beret-wearing fellow who knew everybody and accepted life as the yogi he turned out to be.

In a loaded moment when I judged that a rapport had been forged, I nailed him: "Tell me, Agung, where can I find a balian?" (A balian is a sensitive, or shaman; at least that much I had discovered; there must not be very many of them.)

He paused, turned around and looked at me closely, then with casual innocence said,

"A balian? My wife is a balian."

These Balinese seem to have a way of leaving me speechless, I thought, offering a hurried silent prayer of thanksgiving to the Powers of the Universe for pulling off this breathtaking show of faithfulness . . . and having a divine laugh on the way: My "connection" had been taking us sightseeing.

Recovering, I stammered, "Can I meet her?"

"Yes, of course."

That very evening my husband the good sport and I walked through the balmy tropical night to see my balian. And at the appointed hour we entered the five-hundred-year-old compound of Agung's ancestors. It was of the gray stone and peach brick one sees everywhere in Bali: stately, well proportioned, and with a distinct air of magic to be found just around the corner.

Waiting on the low covered porch stood Rai, Agung's lovely wife, dignified, reserved, smiling: the balian. At the end of this porch, their tiny grinning grandma and her grandson lay on mats watching a loud, clanging Balinese soap opera on TV, like the dance theater we had been enjoying every chance we had. This is also the porch where Agung teaches Yoga classes. "I study, but she just knows," Agung says of his inscrutable wife.

As we sat on the porch floor drinking the Cokes they offered us and exchanging pleasantries, Rai, still composed, drifted quietly into a trance.

"I will tell you what your house looks like in the U.S.," said Rai, before I could protest that it was tree spirits I was after, not a description of something I already knew. Agung scrambled for a scrap of paper and a pen while she tranced out. Presently she began to draw a plan of our rather unusual house: the position of the outbuildings, the gardens, fences, street, and one special tree, the old leaning oak beside my studio, (the other thirty-five trees on our land she ignored).

She couldn't understand why our buildings were at odd angles to each other since in Bali all building complexes are carefully positioned.

"That's right," we marveled. Then I thought, oh, of course, she's proving her skill at 'far sight' so that when she comes to something we don't know we'll be more ready to accept that it also is true. She smiled when we said, "Yes, yes, you've got it all exactly right." She continued, "The old tree leans far out to one side but it is well, and will not soon die." She had answered my unspoken worry about that tree's health. She then correctly picked up on some negative energy flowing towards our land from the west, of which we were well aware.

"Don't worry," she assured us, "The spirits in the big tree have made a wall of fire to protect you."

"A wall of fire? We have a tree spirit? And it protects us?"

"Two spirits," she said firmly. "They watch over you both. They will protect you. They love you and your garden loves you too. There are very good feelings here. Bring presents to them from when you are away to show that you remember."

Presents? I thought of the lovely ritual offerings we saw repeated everywhere throughout Bali. A small flat basket or leaf with flowers and a bit of artfully arranged food is gently placed here or there with a silent prayer and graceful wave of a hand to send the prayer aloft, repeated and renewed daily with the same languid reverence. So the love we have been lavishing on our garden is reciprocated by our own nature spirits.

She then read our auras and energy patterns and prescribed exercises for some minor incipient health problems; then just before we clasped hands to say goodbye, Rai asked, "Questions now?" I asked about the existence of tree spirits, but, perhaps because I was not specific enough, she didn't want to teach me the complicated realm of the unseen. It was late. I would learn of this in the days and months to come.

Besides, we have our own.

"Don't worry," she assured us, "The spirits in the big tree have made a wall of fire to protect you."

After Words

❧ A feng shui (fung shway) expert who had visited us a couple of years before also pointed out this very oak tree as special even with its lost branches and the unsightly gash in its side. Now, there are plenty of other trees on our land; so it seems significant that both sensitives singled out this particular tree. Even this expert had said, "Decorate it." Since then I have offered it the occasional apple or flower, and recently got the notion to arrange small rocks at its base and into the gash, where they remind me to remember.

❧ Interestingly enough, this is the same tree that Alan, the avowed rationalist, has never allowed Randy our arborist, to cut down, regardless of his perfectly good reasons. We have always treated that old oak as a pet. We now call it "the Spirit Tree."

The Solace of Trees

Psychiatrist Viktor E. Frankl tells of a young woman in the same Nazi concentration camp in which he too was imprisoned.

"She knew that she was dying," he says. "Yet she was oddly cheerful, with a kind of triumph over adversity that had been aided by a special tree."

"'This tree that I see through my window is the only friend I have in my loneliness,' she told me. All she could see was . . . one branch of a chestnut tree with two blossoms."

"'I often talk to this tree,'" she said to Dr. Frankl.

"How was I to take her words? Was she delirious? Anxiously I ask, 'Did it answer?'"

"'Yes,' she said."

"'And what did it say?' I asked."

"She replied, 'It said to me, I am here, I am here, I am life, I am eternal life!'"

The German Child

There is another story, this time of Greta, a ten-year old German girl. She was one of many children rushed out of Berlin just before the outbreak of the Second World War. This heroic effort was called *Kindertransport* (the "transport of children") and Greta was sent to live with foster parents in England until the end of the war, whenever that far off day might be.

Though her English foster parents took care of her basic needs, by nature they were cool and reserved and not given to displays of affection. So the child was deprived of the love she had known with her family in Germany and the comforting she craved.

"When the loneliness became unbearable I would run weeping into the garden where grew a big tree," she would later tell. "There, I would throw myself to the ground beneath its outstretched and sheltering branches and cling to its great strong trunk until a loving calmness would come upon me, my tears would dry, and I could bear to go on. Here, I was protected. I loved that tree. It was my only comfort."

Ann's Trees

Ann Fox, the aunt of a friend, told me this story. She was also one of those displaced children of the *Kindertransport.* She was a grown woman when at last she made the journey back to Berlin, the city of her birth.

"All had changed," she said. "My old home was no more. But as I walked around in search of something familiar, I found myself in the park we played in as children. A surge of joy overcame me as I saw the very trees we played among all those many years ago. I recognized them even though they were bigger and had lost limbs. They were the same old friends!"

The solace of trees is there for us when we are in need.

. . . it will never pass into nothingness; but still will keep
A bower quiet for us, and a sleep
Full of sweet dreams, and health, and quiet breathing.

John Keats, *Endymeon*

Why Do We Care So Much?

I have come to believe that there is something so deeply compelling, so personally knowable about trees that it was simply inevitable that trees should be a vital part of our ancestors' creation stories. These were the stories that people told themselves to explain who they were. For instance, there are beautiful Assyrian tablets from 2,300 BCE that show people giving homage to a tree, and an Egyptian wall painting of 1,600 BCE of a sycamore tree with a breast suckling a pharaoh. But there's more going on here than just symbolic pictures and quaint customs.

What would you say if someone whispered into your ear that some of the tree legends and myths were based on real experiences, truths that are still real today? In nearly all places and times, there have been close connections between people and trees.

There was a time when people "spoke" with trees. Even now there are people who can communicate with the natural world. I've had an experience or two myself along these lines that I'll tell you about later. Within these pages, I'll show some evidence that we have spirits and that trees do too. But why do we care so much? Without a doubt there is something powerful and important about trees to explore.

*"Those trees love me,"
Ken Kesey said of
a woods he labored
to save.*

There is a wonderful store of tree knowledge from cultures across the world. The Chinese Healing Masters discovered that when they performed certain exercises, trees could be coaxed to share their immense energy with people. The method of proof was the test of time along with practical results: What worked got used, what didn't work got dropped. And if you happened to be a shaman with the talent, discipline, and spiritual vision required to release a tree's secrets, it worked even better.

We moderns are uncomfortable without a scientific stamp of approval for everything, including trees' importance to the world. So we acknowledge trees' contribution as pollution absorbers, air and water cleaners, coolers, and oxygen makers. But these were not the reasons that the ancients valued trees, though had they known such things they would no doubt have marveled and nodded appreciatively. Of course, they would have known the pleasure of the cooling shade and moister air to be enjoyed beneath the arms of a sheltering tree.

Trees live and die as we do, sometimes living thousands of years and growing to awesome size, concealing within their trunks accurate records of the earth's climatic history. Yet there are, as we shall see, mystical reasons that bond us in comradeship with trees.

"Those trees love me," Ken Kesey said of a woods he labored to save. You believe him. You'd save them too, since a woods of friendly old oaks is preferable to a parking lot, any old day. They can't save themselves, they do us a lot of good, and they look good doing it. We owe them.

There is a thrill of rediscovery when we read mysterious tree lore. Perhaps it nudges memories of the well-loved tree we climbed or played beneath on dreamy summer days; or of a shimmering, rain-spangled tree in a city park.

Did some adventurer from the ancient past cast his reed boat upon the gleaming sea, riding the currents to distant shores, spreading marvelous stories about trees to eager ears? Some of these stories do have a familiar ring. Yet if they had not within them hidden truths, these stories would have blown away like leaves on the wind. Nowadays the legends have come to be regarded merely as charming fairy tales.

There was not, of course, one lone adventurer with the good news about trees.

We know there were great migration paths of peoples moving across the earth, and surely they carried with them cherished tree lore. That lore, transplanted in the fertile soil of the lands they settled, might become reclothed in new exotic raiments, with a branch added here, a rustling there. Cross-cultural seedings happened.

But this cultural exchange doesn't account for those remote, isolated places on earth sprouting their own lively beliefs: traditions of trees as worthies, as gods, as helpers, as healers.

Well, why should we care if the ancient wisdom is preserved or not? Haven't we gone beyond the old stuff and replaced it with up-to-date material? Replaced, yes. Preserved, barely. We need both, to keep balanced and to make life sweet.

Joseph Campbell, the mythologist, said that we need stories to live by. They tell us how it has always been. They tell us the secrets. But we also need new stories to grow on to tell us how to carry on. If we forget, we risk losing our way and our connection with everything and each other. That includes our connection with trees.

How, then, is knowledge preserved and its accuracy maintained? The great skill of memorization and the time-honored art of story telling have the important function of saving precious knowledge. Even today in rural Yugoslavia a story reciter can remember 10,000 lines of verse and will be corrected by the audience if he forgets so much as a single phrase.

The Maoris of New Zealand carefully select and train "memorizers," giving them beautifully carved memory staffs, each notch, each symbol, each spiral representing the *Te Arawa* philosophical understanding of the universe, from creation up to today. The more vivid the imagery, the more the story is impressed on the listener's mind to remember. Legends and myths preserve and keep the lights burning in the lanterns of precious ancient wisdom. We can use the secret treasures they hold or we can ignore them. But if ignored, the message hidden within them dims, darkens and disappears, and those lights blink out forever.

Our shared humanness assures that our senses work pretty much the same way as the next fellow's. So we all have access to universal knowledge. The blind tell us that their missing sense of sight is compensated by the enhancement of their other senses. The psychiatrist Carl Jung believed that there was a source and therefore a resource to what he called the "collective unconscious."

The famous psychic Edgar Cayce said the information is stored in the "akashic records," the psychic reservoir of all the knowledge that ever was.

Fortunately, there have been wise ones among us who have kept ancient wisdom alive for thousands of years, safe from the careless. The time has come to share it.

There was a time when people "spoke" with trees

Why Do We Care So Much?

There have always been those who talk to trees, see their spirits, and know them to be helpers, healers, and power terminals. It is of a reality beyond that which is evident to the five senses, but available, nonetheless, to our subtle senses, a higher octave of our physical senses. It requires only an open heart and faith that there are knowable mysteries beyond, in the world of the unseen.

Once in awhile we get glimpses into another world, a woodland path rarely seen, revealed as if through the melting on a frost-obscured windowpane. The view is so beautiful. Come with me, then, onto that path where people talk with trees and see their spirits. Though the road map is often faint, when we look very carefully we can discover instructions and find help along the way.

My purpose here is not to retell the old stories, which can be found in rich abundance elsewhere; but, rather, as an artist, appreciator, and explorer, to show some hidden truths and to share some mysteries with you, my cousins.

I'll tell you my stories and if, from your experience you will add your own, together we will string our story beads to remind each other of how it is that we are all connected, with people, with trees, and with all that is.

Gradually, then, our senses awaken to the world. We become aware of the thoughts that are thinking all around us . . .and sense the many-voiced forest, listening to us as we speak. And we adjust our own speaking, take new care with our gestures and actions . . . .

David Abram, *The Spell of the Sensuous*

The Healing Masters

Once upon a Chinese time, about 2,600 years ago, there lived a philosopher, a court historian by trade, named Lao Tzu. This honored elder, building upon the wisdom of the past, taught: "Benefit all things . . . treat those who are good with goodness . . . treat those who are not good with goodness . . . repay hatred with virtue . . . . love the earth and be one with Nature;" these and other virtues he taught. (Some of this sound familiar?) He called this the Tao (dow). It means, "The Way."

Following a natural way toward "the One, the Eternal, the Whole" promised a life of peace, harmony, and enlightenment, and followers of The Way were urged to understand and be one with nature. So it was vital to study and closely observe the inner workings of the natural world for clues.

Built upon a long tradition of nature observers whose valuable knowledge had passed down from one to another only by word of mouth, Lao Tzu carefully analyzed then formalized this knowledge to safeguard it.

Before the development of writing, pictographs (picture symbols on stone or wood) were used to preserve precious information. Some pictographs have been found in ancient Chinese tombs showing shamans preparing healing potions from herbs and trees. One picture shows four different kinds of trees used for healing.

There are also ancient stone carvings showing people in dance postures that healers could use for the purpose of correcting physical problems. The postures look exactly like chi gung healing movements used today, and they still work.

Now we come to the art of speaking with trees and using trees' enormous energy to heal people. It is called the Tao of Healing, or Chi Nei Tsung (chee-nay-sung). In this method, highly trained Healing Masters use the universal "vital energy," called *chi.*

The key to the Healing Masters' remarkable abilities is self-mastery, achieved through self-discipline. They rigorously train their minds by practicing meditation and concentration, and train their bodies with specific exercises. They can measure "vital essence" and actually observe the circulation of *chi* energy in things. They can even control energy. But this ability to control things is a great responsibility. These Masters might even be called magicians, tempted to use their skills for selfish purposes since alas, the human ego often gets rapacious, you know, full of itself.

This is where Lao Tzu's philosophy comes in. There were two approaches to The Way: the idealistic wisdom of Lao Tzu, and the Chi Nei Tsung Masters' system of controlling chi. Lao Tzu's wisdom cautions balance, instructing that the manipulation of chi energy is best used for healing.

Since trees are limitless reservoirs of healing power—"power plants," loaded with *chi*—the big news is that even an ordinary person can use *chi,* with a few instructions.

We humans are also "chi containers," but trees churn out *chi* like generators. What's more, trees don't mind being tapped. But how? Let's start with an up-to-date story.

Chinese Tree Healing

The Chi Nei Tsang Masters

Cool morning fog fingered softly through the big trees of San Francisco's Golden Gate Park as a group of eleven martial arts instructors waited in a clearing beyond the footpath. They were dressed in loose white trousers and tunics tied with the black cloth belts indicating their rank as experts. A Chinese Healing Master of the Chi Nei Tsung tradition was coming to instruct them in the ancient art of tree healing: healing with the aid of a tree.

Noiseless as a ghost he stepped from the mists. His straight, fit body masked his considerable age. His calm, noble bearing commanded admiration. The group hushed. He bowed, nodding to each one, and each respectfully returned his bow. They knew his reputation as one who had trained his mind, body, and spirit in the healing arts.

The group of eleven were not without skills of their own. They also had trained rigorously, but in the skills of the warrior where strength and speed are used for self-defense. Their discipline: tae kwon do. They spar by kicking and punching, using feet and hands as weapons. Tae kwon do's code of ethics pledges integrity, courtesy, and self-control. By controlling their minds and bodies, for these experts, it is even possible to

19

break thick boards with the strike of a hand. Tae kwon do began in Korea over 1,000 years ago.

The eleven sat on the ground, listening intently as the master spoke.

"It is possible to receive strength from a tree and use its power to boost your own strength," he began. His voice was strong. "Trees are energy machines. They get food and energy from the earth and sun, and have more than enough for themselves and for you too." His eyes twinkled. Eleven pairs of eyes exchanged glances.

"I trust that the discipline you have gained through your martial arts practices will reward you greatly in this experiment." His smile broadened. "You have been chosen to be here because you have learned the skills of self-control and concentration." His smile turned stern, challenging.

"But what I teach you will not be used for self-defense or attack, my friends. No, it will be used only for healing."

The group knew to wait courteously before asking questions.

"You will use your techniques to control *chi* [chee, or kee] energy. *Chi* is invisible and soundless, like electricity. Chi is the universal vital energy of life. It is in all things: air, water, food, and sunlight. No one doubts that electricity, though invisible, will drive a great machine. And though *chi* is not electricity, when used properly, it has its own power, and like an aura, it is very fine." The eleven knew about *chi*.

Then the master gave them instructions on how to find and befriend a tree.

"Go now. Select a tree and ask its permission. Practice moving *chi* energy in a circle, from the tree to your body and back to the tree, and so on. Meet back here in one hour."

The eleven went off in different directions on their unusual mission. Earlier that same morning they had been practicing stick fighting and leaping.

One young woman, Ms. Lanier (they are addressed formally), was tired and ready for energy from any source, even a tree. She chose an old sycamore tree and leaned heavily against its fawn and white mottled trunk. She was not enthusiastic about this assignment.

Then an odd thing happened to change her mind. After about twenty minutes something began to stir in her. She felt a radiant change in her body energy. *Chi* was gently circulating through her!

Later she told the group, "It was amazing. I sensed that I was being cared for. My entire body became warm with energy and I was no longer tired."

The others told their own stories and reported nurturing from their trees. The old Healing Master beamed, nodding approval of his perceptive students. They bowed courteously to one another and parted to reassemble later.

Some would use this skill again and some would not, but all would remember their tree brothers with new respect.

Afterward, the eleven began another workout session. Ms. Lanier said, "This time I did my strongest work ever, my kicks were more powerful than they had ever been. And as I jumped high, I felt like I was floating!"

Instructions for Tree Healing

Haven't you noticed that you feel better when you're around trees? You breathe more deeply; the air seems cleaner because it actually is cleaner. The Healing Masters say, "Trees can help open our energy channels, cultivate calm, presence, and increase vitality." This is interspecies communication on a very practical level. Let's begin.

How to Collect Tree Chi

First find a tree to work with, a tree buddy. The tree you choose should be big but not too big. It's hard to get the attention of trees that are too big. But don't choose a tree that's too small, because it hasn't enough energy yet to do much good, though small trees are more playful. Select a big strong tree you can relate to, that "feels" just right.

If you have such a tree in your own yard, good. If not, go to some place close to home. Trees growing in parks are good to experiment with because they're used to people being around them. They understand our energy better than trees growing in remote places. Climb your tree if you can, being careful not to hurt it. "These trees would love to have closer relationships with the humans that dominate their environment," says one of the Masters.

Trees can even absorb bad energy. Some Healing Masters are able to observe trees soaking up water and earth-energy through their roots. They can see the beautiful, vital, energy force from heaven flowing through their branches and leaves.

Today a scientist would say: Trees get minerals from the water they draw up from the earth and turn sunlight into food through their leaves,

These trees would love to have closer relationships with the humans that dominate their environment.

Chinese Tree Healing

in photosynthesis. They breathe in carbon dioxide. They breathe out oxygen. They give off water vapor into the air, in transpiration.

Now, humans need the oxygen and water that trees give out in order to live. We breathe out carbon dioxide that trees need to live. This arrangement all happens without our conscious effort and we just take it for granted.

Permission

The Healing Masters say to ask permission before we tap and collect *chi* from a tree. It is considered bad form not to. Trees will gladly give us some of their energy, but we'll need to cultivate the proper techniques, and practice a good attitude to understand their ways. Then a tree's friendship will open up.

Pines, called the "immortal tree," are especially good for healing. They are loaded with *chi* and give off a lot of it. "Pines nourish the blood, strengthen the nervous system, contribute to long life, and nurture souls and spirits," says another Master, with conviction. "One is fortunate indeed to be friends with a pine tree and if the tree is near running water, the energy from the tree is even more powerful."

(A personal note: When house-hunting years ago, my wish went something like this: "pine trees, please, on a sunny knoll with water nearby." As with most strong desires we found such a place. Today those pines are grand old beauties: "sentinels of the South," we call them. Their arms reach wide, their lace-like shade patterns fan the garden, and beneath their glistening needle-clustered boughs, fragrant with pine-pitch, is a quiet place of solace and retreat.)

Approaching and Taking Leave

Having found your tree, introduce yourself to it as you would to a friend. When you leave always thank it, a ritual of quiet communion. (If you can't say it, think it.) It is a way to keep mindful of the special connection you are making, a reverent ceremony setting up harmony between you

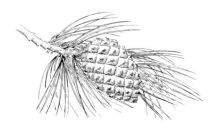

and your tree. Energy is subtle, so to sense it, you'll need to let go of your critical eyes, using "soft" eyes instead. (Practice will help.)

Breathe calmly for a few minutes. (You can stand or sit, but come to rest near the trunk.) Get a feel for the tree. Enjoy the peacefulness. Visualize a gentle, warm light coming from the tree to your heart. Now flow it into your body and down into the earth and back into the tree. Then flow it up the tree and back to yourself again.

It becomes a cycle of gentle, healing light. It feels very soothing and refreshing. You have now done an energy exchange. You have a partner, a friend. The more you meet with your tree, the deeper the friendship. The more you practice, the deeper the bond. In time, you may even see this *chi* light.

Every tree has a life force of its own. Some trees are very generous and want to give you all the energy you can take. Some are just friendly souls who enjoy human company. Others are weak or ill and could use some of your comforting, healing energy to open up their blockages. Still others are quite indifferent to you. Experiment, be patient, learn, be respectful. Don't be demanding. Trees live on a different time scale than humans; so allow enough time for results. Return to your tree to establish rapport. Let your tree know that it can look forward to seeing you again.

The best time to practice connecting with your tree is in the morning before noon.

Pines nourish the blood, strengthen the nervous system, contribute to long life, and nurture souls and spirits.

Here Is Another Way

Get quiet. Offer a greeting. Assume an open, friendly attitude. Stand with palms upward about two feet from your tree. When the tree responds with its energy, draw it in and "breathe" it into your body with thankful calmness. Repeat several times. Take your time. Let your intuition guide you. (In Western terms, this is sometimes called "running energy," you'll get what it means.) Observe what happens. Practice training your mind to move and guide the *chi*. A circulating exchange of energy will happen from the tree to you and back.

When the Healing Masters are working on specific health problems, counting the number of circulation exchanges is important. But for our purposes it can get a little distracting remembering the count (let's see, was that thirty-five or thirty-six cycles I counted?) Counting restricts the natural, free-flowing intuitive process; getting anxious could spoil the fun.

Chinese Tree Healing

It helps to invent and repeat a simple phrase to clear those busy thoughts from your head. For example: "*chi,* flow free, between me and my tree." Simple, but memorable.

When it's time to withdraw, close off with a crisp ending gesture, a smooth upward arc, then a little downward punch, saying "Ho!" or "Amen." That's it.

Of course for serious problems it is the Healing Masters' careful and painstaking methods that enabled them to get their remarkable results. This is described by a practitioner I know as the "Wow!" effect.

Here's a way to clean and brighten your aura: Sit in meditation with your back to your tree, absorbing its energy. This will take away any drab grayness from your own energy field.

In time, you can ask your tree for healing from a distance, to refine your energy and improve your health.

After Words

- Once, when hiking with friends in Yosemite National Park, I experienced this healing, though I knew nothing then of Chi Nei Tsung. I slipped down an incline, painfully turning my ankle. We stopped by a big fir tree awhile, but the pain persisted. Not wanting to hold things up for the others, the thought came to embrace that beautiful tree. Silently I asked it to lend me its strength and please float some of its energy under my steps for the remaining two miles back to Camp Curry. Wonderfully, it granted my wish. The pain vanished. My mantra that day was, "thank you, thank you, thank you." Every time I remember that kindly old fir tree, I well up.

- Trees and other plants create negative ions: good. But city sidewalks create positive ions: bad. So says the Dutch yogi, Jack Schwarz. This is yet another reason parks and forests are so important to us, as retreats for reenergizing and for nourishing our souls. (Schwarz, 1974)

Which Heals What

According to the Chi Nei Tsung Masters, some trees are warm, some are hot, some are cool, and others cold. Try distinguishing one type of tree from another to see what the properties are of each. Practice will improve your skills. (Good intuition training)

Banyan: Clears heart, helps rid body of dampness.

Birch: Helps clear heat and dampness from body, helps detoxify body.

Cinnamon: Clears coldness from heart and abdomen.

Cypress: Reduces heat. Nourishes yin energy.

Cedar: Reduces heat. Nourishes yin energy.

Elm: Calms the mind, strengthens stomach.

Fir: Helps clear up bruises, reduces swelling, heals broken bones faster.*

Fig: Clears excess heat from body, increases saliva, nourishes spleen, helps stop diarrhea.

Ginkgo: Helps strengthen bladder and alleviate urinary problems in women.

Hawthorne: Aids digestion, strengthens intestines, lowers blood pressure.

Locust: Helps clear internal heat, helps balance weather of heart.

Maple: Chases sick winds, helps reduce pain.

Pine: Powerful, nurtures souls and spirits; radiates *chi,* nourishes blood, nervous system, promotes long life.

Plum: Nourishes spleen, stomach, pancreas, calms the mind.

Willow: Expels sick winds, rids body of excess dampness, reduces high blood pressure, strengthens urinary tract and bladder.

- *Note:* I found it remarkable that the fir tree in my experience is the tree I intuitively called upon for help with a sprained, bruised foot.
- Investigate first; ask an herbologist or your druggist for advice.

Gaia

I smiled on hearing of the Gaia hypothesis: "The earth is a living being." I pictured the earth from space as the astronauts had seen it when first standing on the moon: a glowing blue ball, rolling through the solar system, vanilla cream clouds swirling over pistachio green landmasses. Zeroing in, I could almost hear its lungs gently breathing, its heart rhythmically beating, and the lights of cities twinkling. I could see its teeming life forms appearing through the parting clouds and watch the trees perform their mesmerizing magic of changing sunlight, carbon dioxide, and water into food, then give off water vapor into the air: photosynthesis, respiration, and transpiration. Meanwhile bees are pollinating flowers and everything is interacting with everything else in an intricate dance of mutual benefit to all. And in the background are strains of Pythagoras' "music of the spheres." A sweet story, but what's the reality? What really happened back in July, 1969 when *Apollo 11* went to the moon?

We remember fondly what the astronauts said after being out there in space: "I was overwhelmed with a divine presence . . . and saw the earth and the universe as an intelligent system," said one. "I fell in love with the earth," said another. "I found God on the moon," said a third.

When the space program rocketed humans off our planet into space it shook us awake. This audacious adventure presented humankind with earnest questions. We wanted new explanations for our little blue island's place in the universe.

Meanwhile, the big question that had been driving NASA and the Jet Propulsion Laboratory was: Is there life on Mars? But the spotlight switched from Mars to Earth, however, once we all laid our eyes on those knockout pinup pictures of Earth from space. We were in love. Everybody was so dazzled by the sheer beauty of our gorgeous little home planet that the life-on-Mars question shifted into second place.

For the first time in history, human beings were seeing Earth as *outsiders*. It was absolutely thrilling. Being outside made all the difference in our awareness. We could clearly see that Earth was unique among the planets in our neat little solar system; the other planets looked drab and dead while Earth looked alive.

. . . the findings were too bizarre and far out for comfort

So in 1961, NASA hired Dr. James Lovelock, a biologist and atmospheric scientist, as a consultant and team member to investigate, and Dr. Lynn Margulis joined the team.

The burning question then became: Why are the gases that make up Earth's atmosphere of such an unlikely mix? What on earth is happening here? The search for answers was on, and in the end, the findings were too bizarre for comfort. They seemed downright unscientific. Scientists fidgeted and wore pained expressions. You see, Earth was behaving just like a living being.

Fascinated with their discoveries and undaunted by the seemingly unscientific implications, Lovelock and Margulis formulated a hypothesis. They proposed a charming and poetic way to think about it all, calling their hypothesis, "Gaia," named after the Greek goddess who gathered the living world out of chaos. Earth acted alive.

Now, a living being is described as a self-regulating living system. A living being acts in its own interest. Strangely enough this describes exactly what Earth does. Because of Earth's odd atmospheric mix of chemicals, it is forced to balance, transform, and maintain itself. It is living. Aha.

"Earth's surface is . . . made fit and comfortable by the presence of life itself," said Lovelock, "from whales to viruses, oaks to algae, [it] could be regarded as constituting a single living entity . . . with powers beyond its seeming capacity."

Earth Lives!

Here's how it works: Everything is maintained and kept balanced by active feedback processes. Earth adjusts to changes in order to keep itself alive. "Increased diversity leads to better regulation," says Margulis. So the more different kinds of species there are, the better their chances of surviving. Furthermore, any species that is bad for the environment is doomed, while anything that helps the environment is, in turn, helped and flourishes. Reassuring, wouldn't you say? "Evolution is the result of cooperative, not competitive processes," says Margulis. Then it is not just survival of the fittest, as Darwin supposed?

Now that is something to think about.

But we humans have a way of meddling with nature for our own sake. Nature doesn't need humans and could get along very well without us. But we need nature. So since the burning of fossil fuels is harmful to the atmosphere, we might instead choose alternatives such as sun power, wind power, water power, and the like, to drive our engines. Why couldn't we let those choices be our respectful gift to the Earth and to the coming generations? Why not?

The breath of Earth is the breath of life. It is the interaction of all that exists on our planet. And its heartbeat is our own.

After Words

❧ "We are part of the earth and it is part of us." (Chief Seattle, 1854)

❧ "If, in fact, the Earth does function as a living organism, then human activity that disrupts the biochemistry of that organism can lead to grave consequences. . . . The massive burning of fossil-fuel energy is the first example of human activity on a global scale that now threatens a radical shift in the climate of the Earth and the undermining of the biosphere that sustains all living creatures. . . . There are rare moments in history when a generation of human beings are given a new gift to rearrange their relationship to one another and the world around them. This is such a moment." (Rifkin, 2003)

❧ "A man's attitude towards Nature is of special importance because as we respect our created world, so also do we show respect for the real world that we can't see." (Thomas Yellowtail, 1903–1993, Crow Indian medicine man)

❧ "I now believe what we should have said was: The whole system of life and its material environment is self-regulating at a state comfortable for the organism.". . . The discovery of dimethyl sulfide as a key compontent of the natural environment was the first useable prediction for Gaia. (Lovelock, 1995)

❧ "Whether right or wrong, Gaia provides a very different, a top-down, view of our planet, in a world where science grows ever more conservative and dogmatic. I think we need to make room for the kind of errors that leads us closer to the truth. As the economist Vilfredo Pareto said, 'Give me a fruitful error any time, full of seeds, bursting with its own corrections'." (Lovelock, 1992)

The Cosmic Tree

Haven't we all wondered where we came from and why we're here? Is there a Big Plan? And, if so, why weren't we given instructions or at least a map with directions to the exit? Well, yes, there is this death-of-the-body business, the final "snuff" and then goodbye . . . but is that all there is?

We were not the first to have asked these questions of course. Many thousands of years ago our ancient ancestors puzzled over them, too, and came up with some ingenious ways of explaining important concepts so that anybody could understand them at a glance. Pictures did the trick, and one of the simplest recognizable images was a tree. But, actually, it's a diagram masquerading as a tree. It's called the Cosmic Tree, or Tree of Life. Add a little story, and you've got a lasting instruction device that transfers down through the ages. The tree symbol is found all over the world.

The big message this tree symbol describes is that there is a source, a sacred center from which all-that-is began. This "still point" from which all creation springs is called the axis mundi: "turning point of the world: line through the earth's center around which the universe revolves." Let me explain from an artist's point of view.

Where We Came From

Imagine that you are about to doodle on a piece of clean, white paper. You select a big black pencil and draw a big black dot. The dot sits there quietly as you think what to draw next. Then you notice something stirring within the dot. You see, looking closely, that crammed into that black dot is everything that exists in the whole, entire universe; only all-things-existing can't get out of the dot and are wriggling impatiently to be set free. Of course, you want to help them out; so, pretending that you are God, you say to Yourself in omnipotent voice: *"I shall create a place for them."*

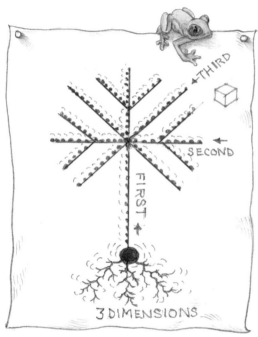

So, you draw a line vertically up from that dot. All at once you have created a place in space . . . a *dimension.* Immediately everything becomes visible and begins scrambling out of the dot and up the line as fast as they can, eager to arrange themselves according to their specialties. But they can't quite do that yet because they need a horizontal line to crawl sideways on. So, you draw a horizontal line across the vertical line. Aha, you've done it again. You have created a *second* dimension. Now everything scurries out on this line, expectantly; but something's still missing.

You stand back, frown, then smiling, step forward to draw some more horizontal lines to the back and to the front of the vertical line (use your imagination.) Congratulations, you have just created a *third* dimension. The lines are spaced out nicely since you like balance, order, and drawing stick figures is your specialty.

Quick as a flash everything zips this way and that, finding exactly the perfect little niche, very happy indeed to have a place to be. You smile again, pleased with yourself, saying, *"That was good"* (because that's sort of what God always says after creating something. (See *Genesis 4.*)

Well, that in a nutshell is how it all began. Just a quick sketch, of course.

Examining the drawing further, you think, "It looks like a tree, it has a vertical trunk and horizontal branches. All it needs are roots." So quickly you draw a few root lines at the bottom, and are quite pleased with yourself for creating such an easy to grasp, friendly symbol. You announce, *"I shall call it: the Cosmic Tree."*

As you gaze admiringly at your tree, it occurs to you that it nicely symbolizes certain important concepts. The trunk, rising from its roots in the mysterious Underworld, passes through the Earth plane where we all live, and stretches its branches to Heaven above: three different planes—Underworld, Earth, and Heaven. These are symbolic clues, leading us to answers for the big questions of "where," "what," and "why." It is a diagram we can quickly refer to when the day's work is done and we pause to ponder.

Since you are in a creative frenzy, like visual aids, and enjoy playing God, you say to Yourself, *"I shall now demonstrate this idea of separate planes."* (Planes are a way of explaining that there are different levels, states, or realms of consciousness.)

So, on a fresh paper you draw a simple vertical line (representing a tree) then draw three pancakes (planes) skewered on it with spaces between to separate them. See? Planes. You glance around to see if anyone has noticed your rare depth of creative acuity.

So, now we can see more clearly how these planes are separate from each other. It is the tree that connects them, and the tree that allows access from one plane to the next. Theoretical physicists say that there are many more planes. So did the ancients. Well then, you simply add more "pancakes" to the stack on the stick, each one defining a separate plane. I'll explain more later. Now just sit back, fold your arms, and watch the fun. Observe what you have set loose from that one black dot.

What follows is a wondrous bursting forth of creative energy differentiating into the most fabulous variety of forms imaginable: Life!

Pause a moment to contemplate those eternal questions—"where?" "what?" and "why?"—and reflect on all the people who have ever asked them. The ancient creators of the Cosmic Tree were none other than our own kin from an earlier time, not much different, and capable of abstract thoughts way beyond "What's for lunch?"

Through the years the concept of the Cosmic Tree has been ingeniously expanded and embellished. Vivid stories and myths have been told to explain how life began. Pictures have been painted, symbols have been modeled in clay, carved in wood and stone, woven into story tapestries, and measured into music, stories, songs, and dances all with great meaning. The Cosmic Tree was encoded into temples and shrines

What follows is a wondrous bursting forth of creative energy differentiating into the most fabulous variety of forms imaginable: Life!

The Cosmic Tree

in what is called sacred geometry, because it has a meaning beyond the ordinary. All this was to keep people mindful, lest they forget.

Right from the start, trees, poles, and mountains with ladders or steps to climb them symbolized ascension to higher planes. Usually seven to ten in number, they made the planes easy to get to.

There are beautiful examples of sacred geometry in Buddhist temple-shrines. Their thin "steeples" display seven spaced disks, like our pancakes-skewered-on-a-stick, a sacred concept transformed into architecture. People could easily see at a glance the concept of the different planes. And it is the pole, tree, or "skewer" that serves as the all-important connector between the planes.

In Japan there are elegant shrines of great height built of "houses" stacked one upon another, each "house story" a little smaller as they rise, each containing sacred relics: five to seven complete houses demonstrating in 3-D the idea of different planes. Some say the stacking was merely a way to attain a high building. But one can easily imagine climbing up and visiting each house to explore its special qualities and its secrets. (While one is in the altered state of consciousness called meditation, it is possible to experience these planes.)

Thousands of unique, breathtaking examples of art and architecture across the world have been created to show the rest of us how to understand these complex concepts, food to feed the hungry soul.

These brilliant visual interpretations have sprung from the beating hearts and thoughtful minds of ingenious human beings, rapping urgently on our windows to tell us there is a way to climb the Cosmic Tree towards the reward of enlightenment. They tell the ongoing story of ever knowing, ever expanding creation.

You could say we are co-creators with the Creator, telling the creation story through our own creative ingenuity. And as such, are guardians of this precious world. A cause for rejoicing, wouldn't you say?

After Words

❧ "The center is, first and foremost, the point of 'absolute beginning' where the latent energies of the sacred first broke through . . . ultimately all creation takes place at this point which represents the ultimate source of reality . . . .often referred to as the 'navel of the world,' 'divine egg,' 'Hidden Seed' or 'Root of Roots' . . . it is also imagined as a vertical axis, the 'cosmic axis' or 'axis of the world' (Axis Mundi) which stands at the center of the universe. . . ." (Cook, 1988)

❧ "The imagination is a tree . . . it lives between earth and sky." (Gaston Bachelard, French philosopher, cited in Cook, 1988)

What Is the Root?

What
Is the
Root of all these
Words?

One Thing: Love

But a love so deep and sweet
It needed to express itself
With scents, sounds, colors
That never before
Existed

Hafiz (Sufi Master, 1320-1389) from *The Gift*

Groves of Power

King of the Woods

W ho would guess that a setting so tranquil could hide so dark a story? Placid little lake Nemi rests within the Alban hills just a few miles from Rome. There, in ancient times, above its northern shore stood a splendid temple of power, dedicated to the great goddess of all Nature, Diana. Its white marble columns and descending terraces reflected across the lake's glassy surface like a mirror: "Diana's mirror."

A silvery spring splashed from a grotto that fed the lake, its clear waters passing close by a huge sacred oak tree, the most sacred of all the trees in Diana's Sacred Grove. The oak wore a garlanded skirt encircling its trunk, glinting with little crescent moons. The vestal priestesses tended it as carefully as they tended the sacred, ever-burning fire.

Wild animals roamed around the lake and drank from its cool waters. Birds flitted through the trees and small creatures scurried about. All protected by Diana.

For countless years people had been making pilgrimages to this temple and its sacred grove, paying tribute, leaving offerings, and, in return, asking favors, such as abundant crops or many children.

But there were rules to obey. No one would dare touch or pluck even a twig of the sacred tree for fear of being punished by its guardian priest, known as King of the Woods. He was intermediary between tree and petitioner.

Grimly, this priest-king patrolled the land around the tree both day and night. Though he wore a fine gold wreath upon his helmet and a sword belt around his waist with sheath wonderfully carved in magical figures, he did not smile. Ever suspicious of intruders, his hand rarely strayed from the hilt of his sword that must be ready to strike down the murderer he knew would one day come to kill him, just as he had killed the priest-king before him. For this was the only way a new priest could replace the old one!

This dark deadly drama had been repeating for hundreds of years.

Incredibly, the challenger must always be a slave. A warrior perhaps, or gladiator captured in battle. He must prove his superior strength and cunning by sneaking past the priest-king. Then he had to climb the sacred tree, pluck the magic mistletoe growing amongst its highest branches, carrying it back with him to the ground without being detected: a deadly game, indeed.

If the thieving slave were successful in eluding the priest-king and snatching the mistletoe, he became entitled to challenge the priest-king in a fight to the death. Then, if triumphant, he would himself become King of the Woods!

We can almost see the older priest-king waiting in the shadowy dusk as the light of day fades away. Would this be the night, or tomorrow, or when? He is alert as always, heart pounding, nerves twitching, clenching the hilt of his sword, desperate to kill the expected intruder as he himself had killed those many years before. A twig snaps. The priest-king's trained but dimming eyes search the gloom.

Suddenly a ragged man, armed with sharp-edged rocks drawn from his belt-pouch, drops from the tree to the ground, springs up, and charges. A practiced marksman, he moves in swiftly, mistletoe clutched in one hand, jagged rock hefted in the other. And rotating his body like an uncoiling snake, he hurls the rock, striking the priest-king's brow dead on. In his pain the priest-king's sword slips from his hand. The slave, seizing it, thrusts it deep into the side of the doomed priest, who falls to the earth, his life seeping away with his blood, adding its life-giving strength to the sacred soil.

The victorious slave is now King of the Woods to rule and defend his power until he himself is killed. And so, next year, and the next, sooner or later, the fateful day must come when the deadly ritual is once again acted out.

It is in this way, and only this way, that the title passed to a successor!

Exactly why it was necessary to kill the King of the Woods is hidden within the dim folds of time. We might guess that a sacred temple required

. . . his sword that must be ready to strike down the murderer he knew would one day come to kill him, just as he had killed the priest-king before him

constant safeguarding from thieves (always a threat). And a proven, powerful priest-king would command fear and respect. The question of the suitability of a former slave in the role of priest could be of secondary importance to his role as feared protector. A slave might even buy his own freedom by volunteering for such an act. He could be taught the rules of the system as well as another could.

Besides, being the priest-king carried enormous prestige, honor, and wealth, although it wasn't exactly an enviable job, and everybody knew how he would die. So a slave had nothing to lose and much to gain.

Beyond protection, why was it so necessary that a priest-king speak for the sacred tree? Why not let the tree spirit speak for itself in its own whispery ways, as it used to when people lived closer to nature and shamans spoke with certain powerful trees? Well, isn't it simply more practical to worship a real person rather than to wait patiently for supernatural signs like leaf-rustlings to announce the presence of an invisible tree god? Perhaps it comes down to practicality: A human being conveniently speaks your language; so he or she can "interpret" tree-talk.

Considering the priest-king's fight to power, it is unlikely that there was anything magical about him beyond the form of his protection service, that is, unless he believed that magical powers were bestowed on him when he took over the office of priest-king.

The priest-king's duty was to represent the tree's spirit. Say, for instance, that a petitioner wants a favor from the tree spirit; rain for his crops, maybe. So he gives an offering to the priest-king who then performs a ritual or exchanges a "rain-charm." If it rains, the petitioner's offering was acceptable. But if no rain, the offering must have been lacking something; so a more potent sacrifice or offering might be required, or so the reasoning might go.

Why not let the tree spirit speak for itself in its own whispery ways, as it used to when people lived closer to nature and shamans spoke with certain powerful trees?

Yet we shouldn't undervalue the power of belief in a pilgrim's mind. Belief works.

Regardless of how the petitioner thought about the transaction, wasn't it more useful to deal with a real person than a tree spirit? A real person could trade a comforting "rain-charm" for a few coins, whereas a tree spirit has no pockets.

The first priest-king of Nemi was a fellow named Verbius (whose real name was Hippolytus.) Diana appointed him priest-king because she loved him. He even became a minor deity. Of course he must never be touched because he represented the sun.

Ancient votive offerings and "fertility charms" have been found at Nemi showing Diana in her later, gentler form, worshiped as protector of women for conception and safe delivery. But originally she was known as a woodland goddess and a tree spirit. She was mistress of forest creatures and domestic animals.

But the awesome power of nature itself was the older, deeper drama, even before the King of the Woods came to the sacred grove. Wild, raw, pitiless nature was symbolized by the wrath of Artemis, the mythological Greek goddess. She terrified people.

It was the Bronze-Aged Minoans of Crete, 3000-1000 BCE, who called her Diana the Huntress. Heart-clutching fear underlay Diana's tree cult. It was she who demanded death to any stranger with the audacity to tempt nature's awesome power. Woe unto him! The threat was reason enough in those scary old days.

The great trees in Nemi's sacred grove represented nature's largest and oldest living things on earth. The power within trees could light up the sun and bring rain; after all, was it not well known that fire was contained in the wood of trees? Any fool knew that trees stored fire as they stored sap. One need only rub two dry twigs together and pretty soon fire would burst forth. Is this not proof?

The famous "golden bough" plucked from Nemi's sacred grove was not a bough at all, but the mysterious mistletoe, most magical of plants. Though it nestles in trees it seems to appear from thin air, and remains alive separate from its tree-host. What's more, potions can be made from mistletoe for mysterious purposes.

Some might question that mistletoe was the golden bough, but no one questions mistletoe's great importance in the ancient world.

A real person could trade a comforting "rain-charm" for a few coins, whereas a tree spirit has no pockets.

After Words

❧ Proof of the temple's power and wealth comes from the emperor Octavian. In the year 31 BCE he borrowed cash from the temple because it was richer than he was.

❧ There is a worldwide tradition of kings as deities, spokesmen for the gods, the go-between connecting man and god. It still exists today. The Emperor Hirohito of Japan, as late as 1946, was thought to be a divinity. When we hear the phrase "the king is dead, long live the king!," does Nemi come to mind?

❧ The story King of the Woods, here told, was inspired by Frazer's classic work, *The Golden Bough.* It is but one story of one sacred grove from the thousands spread across the ancient lands of the world. The sacredness of trees was an unquestioned fact.

❧ "Sympathetic magic" comes to mind when we think of substitutes. For instance, a hunter makes an effigy of a deer he plans to hunt, paints some magical marks on it, offers prayers, even thanks the deer's spirit. Later, if the deer is hunted and killed, the effigy is proven a successful substitute for the deer. The magic works. If it doesn't work, the hunter will just have to make a better effigy.

❦ In a parallel line of thought, J. G. Frazer tells the story of a Cambodian hunter who has set his nets for game but has caught nothing: "He strips himself naked, then strolls up to the net, becomes entangled, and in mock surprise cries, 'Hillo! What's this? I'm afraid I'm caught!'" The net having got the idea is now sure to catch game. If not, the hunter will just have to add a bit more magic into his ritual.

❦ The magical, mystical Druids (from roots meaning both "oak" and "he who knows") also had sacred groves. Druids were a powerful force of the British Isles and Gaul, BCE. To them the oak symbolized the supreme deity. Druid priests were highly regarded physicians, theologians, philosophers, poets, and wisdom-keepers of their time. They were also the highest political authorities. It was the Druid high priest who climbed the great oak to cut the magic mistletoe with a golden sickle.

❦ The Druids of Britain even devised an alphabet encoded with the special meanings of trees. The characters of the alphabet were described as "twig" or "branch" letters. The writing was called "Bobileth" or "tree writing," and each character was named after a tree. Ah, those Druids! A scholar, Lewis Spence, reminds us, "To the man who has no magic in his blood, the cavern of Celtic profundity is forever sealed." (Spence, 1994; Hall, 1972)

❦ A possible explanation for the killing of the king comes from a time when, for over 25,000 years the Goddess religion was practiced. It was She who was regarded as the Supreme Creator. Inheritance passed from mother to daughter or through the female line, thereby keeping title to property. The wealthy temples of the Goddess-Queen lasted as long as an ambitious would-be priest-king didn't get a notion to start his own religion. It was a remarkably egalitarian and peaceful chapter in human history. (Stone, 1976; Eisler, 1987)

❦ The holy fire at Nemi's grove required rituals, purifications, and sacrifices. Exactly the right number of vestal virgins (up to six, within historic times) tended and watched the perpetual fire, which must never go out. Oak wood was plentiful, made a good, hot, long-burning fire, and since from sun comes heat, the oak tree was favored by the sun.

❦ "My Destiny waits for the freeman as well as him enslaved by another's might." (Aeschylus, 525-456 BCE)

❦ I'd searched for hours for pictures of golden mistletoe, got fed up and went for a hike with Alan. We found a good rest spot under an oak, and looking up, I yelled, "Look! Mistletoe, and it's golden!" Alan-the-tall fished it down for me. Blessed again. You can see it in the illustration that begins this story and the one on the previous page.

The Druids of Britain even devised an alphabet encoded with the special meanings of trees. The characters of the alphabet were described as "twig" or "branch letters."

The King of the Woods

Sacred Groves

The Safe Havens

Have you ever entered a sun-dappled wood, felt a hush, and sensed within the stillness something beyond the ordinary . . . a feeling of the sacred? That, at its simplest, is the effect of a sacred grove. The ancients knew them well.

What exactly is a grove? Unlike the vast, dark forests that once nearly covered the earth, tangled and impassable, a grove of trees has no undergrowth; it's a clearing within a wood that is passable or even habitable. It is a sheltered place, a safe haven away from the dangers of exposed lands in a hostile world. A grove, then, was the perfect place for a sanctuary. A well-chosen grove would be the perfect spot where the natural and supernatural meet. Here in its green silence, one could encounter a deity. Here is where the first altars were erected to woodland gods and tree spirits.

The Old German word for "temple" derives from the same word as "grove."

But the same trees that provided safety and protection by daylight became sinister in the deepening shadows of night, for who knew what mysterious forces lurked in a night-forest. The looming presence of massive thousand-year-old trees, their mighty limbs shrouded in slow-moving mists, could strike terror in the hearts of short-lived humans who revered, yet feared them. Legends were passed from parent to child of certain ever-watchful trees, harboring malevolent spirits. They must be appeased.

Careful rituals must be devised, with offerings and sacrifices placed on the altar to coax alliance of a tree spirit or nature god in a perilous world.

How Can We Know?

How can we know with any certainty what went on in the minds of our prehistoric ancestors? Clues from scholars can help us trace their tracks. But first, let's start by comparing our similarities, so we can get connected with their distant heartbeats.

We still have religions with rituals, and sacred places called, among other things, temples, churches, and mosques in which to perform them. We have sacred objects and chants, meaningful repetitive phrases. These are formulas designed for connecting us with the unseen or divine.

Here's what's necessary for religion to exist, according to anthropologist E. B. Tylor: "In the absence of written records, [human] processes and reactions can be used to reconstruct the past. Supernaturalism is a minimum requirement for religion . . . a definition of religion is belief in a spiritual being. . . . Animism is in fact the groundwork of the philosophy of religion."

Sanskrit scholar F. Max Muller says, "The impulse to religious thought and language arises . . . from sensuous experience, external nature . . . surprise, terror, marvels, miracles, the vast domain of the infinite:" things like sun, fire, rain, wind, and strange places like caves.

This all seems perfectly logical; otherwise, why would we still have the urge to keep these rituals going? If there were no need, we'd have abandoned these things as unnecessary. But marvels and miracles do still happen. And we need a labeled box to put them in, which our ancestors conveniently provided, with their sacred groves, altars, and rituals. Besides, the stuff works.

Shamans were the go-betweens. They were those special people with the talent and spiritual sensitivity to do the job of connecting with the unseen. But calling up and repeating miracles is chancy. So rituals had to be created to increase the chances for success. Effective rituals induced an altered-state-of-consciousness in the shaman. Rituals, being ordered patterns, provided just the formulas to get the desired results. And the ancients went to a lot of trouble devising just the right procedures. But certain needs had to be satisfied first.

For instance, psychologist Abraham Maslow describes a "hierarchy of needs." Visualize the hierarchy as a pyramid: At its broad base are the most basic *physical* needs, such as air, water, food, sleep. Next come the needs for *safety,* security, and protection. Next come *emotional* needs, belonging and love. Next come *social* needs, connecting to society. Last come *aesthetic* needs, which includes religion and art. Before the top ones can be expressed, the needs at the base of the pyramid must be satisfied.

So sacred groves, attending to our needs for safety, belonging, society, and religion just about take care of all our basic needs. So far, so good. Yet the need for religious experience was always awaiting fulfillment, because we needed a source for controlling our *destiny.*

Sacred Groves and the Worship of Trees

No question that connecting with the unseen has been a universal pursuit for countless thousands of years.

There is also a widely held notion that the world is animate, that life pulses in everything including rocks and rivers. Today this concept is brought forward by the science of quantum physics, which has come to the same conclusion as the ancients. Quite intriguing. Personally, this view becomes more attractive with the passing years. It's sort of friendly, inclusive, and nothing's excluded.

Now let's review some examples of famous groves and places.

Perhaps the oldest of all Greek sanctuaries was Dodona, where Zeus, king of all gods, "spoke" by rustling the leaves of his sacred oaks, especially in the highest places.

In Rome his name was Jupiter. The root of the names Zeus and Jupiter means "shining" and "bright" like the lightning bolts hurled by Zeus. It follows then, that oak trees are where sun and fire were kept. Grand ceremonies were celebrated to "cause the sun to shine and the fruits of the earth to grow."

Other spirits were recognized as existing too. They ranged from lesser up to the ranks of powerful deities. It was understood that spiritual

There is also a widely held notion that the world is animate, that life pulses in everything including rocks and rivers.

Sacred Groves

beings controlled our lives both here and hereafter, and that our actions pleased or displeased the gods. So one had better make offerings and do it properly, carefully following set rituals. This is a recurring theme across the world.

For instance: In ancient Prussia, the reverence for and worship of sacred oaks was central to the peoples' religion. The greatest sacred tree was in the holy grove of Romov. It was the special dwelling place of a god. There, a hierarchy of priests tended and kept watch over a perpetual fire made of oak wood. The tree was kept veiled with a cloth, removed only on special occasions to allow worshipers to see the tree.

It is so common a practice across the world to appease the soul of a tree and ask its forgiveness for doing it harm, that there is no question about its importance. Here are some examples of famous groves from literally thousands:

- In the old religious capital of Sweden at Uppsala, there was a sacred grove in which every tree was considered divine. Human sacrifices were made there.

- "When a grove is sacred and inviolable, it is so because it is believed to be either inhabited or animated by sylvan deities," says J. G. Frazer, who also says, "in Lavonia, there is a sacred grove in which, if any man fells a tree or even breaks a branch, he will die within a year."

- Frazer tells the story of a Russian Wotjak "who ventured to hew a tree from one of their sacred groves, fell sick and died the next day."

- Cato wrote, "Before thinning a grove, a Roman farmer had to sacrifice a pig to the god or goddess of the grove."

- In Japan, Shinto shrines are located in small groves with at least one sacred tree, the home of a *kami,* a divine spirit. The tree is tied around with a sacred rope, which designates it as special.

- Pliny (CE 27-89) wrote, "In the Roman Forum, busy center of Roman life, the sacred fig tree of Romulus was worshiped, down to the days of the empire. The withering of its trunk was enough to bring consternation through the city."

- "On Rome's Palatine Hill," wrote Plutarch (first century CE), "grew a cherry tree that was esteemed one of the most sacred objects in Rome. Whenever the tree appeared to a passerby to be drooping, he set up a hue and cry, which was echoed by the people in the street, and soon

It is so common a practice across the world to appease the soul of a tree and ask its forgiveness for doing it harm, that there is no question about its importance.

a crowd might be seen running from all sides with buckets of water as if hastening to put out a fire."

- Siamese Buddhist monks say that there are souls everywhere, and to destroy anything whatever is to forcibly dispossess a soul. They will not break even a branch of a tree, "as one would not break the arm of an innocent person."

- The Dyaks of Borneo assign souls to trees and will not dare cut down an old tree.

- The Ojibwa Indians seldom cut down green or living trees, from the idea that it puts them to pain. Some of their medicine men profess to have heard the wailing of the trees under the axe, writes Peter Jones.

- When an oak is being felled, "It gives a kind of shriek or groan that may be heard a mile off, as if it were the genius of the 'oake' lamenting," reports J. Aubrey.

- The Battas of Sumatra have been known to refuse to cut down certain trees because they were the abode of mighty spirits who would resent the injury.

- The Churka Coles of India say that the tops of trees are inhabited by spirits, disturbed by the cutting down of the trees, and will take vengeance.

- On the Japanese island of Hokkaido, the earliest people there, known as the Ainu, had a tree cult the name of which translates as "the Doctrine of Preservation by Trees." They determined their lives with help from different kinds of trees. They bowed to and deified the forces of nature. Among the Ainus, "good trees" are the ash, oak, spruce, alder, birch, yew, chestnut, willow, dogwood, magnolia, hornbeam, and mulberry, all homes of deities.

- Not long ago in Africa's Congo, holy trees were planted in front of each village house, and jars of wine placed under them as offerings to the tree's spirit.

- The huge silk-cotton tree (*Ciba pentandra*) houses a deity; so it is protected from cutting or disfiguring.

- The Wanika of eastern Africa say that every tree has its spirit. Trees have souls like their own, and they treat them with great respect.

The Wanika of eastern Africa say that every tree has its spirit. Trees have souls like their own, and treat them with great respect.

Sacred Groves

- When I was in Bali, I saw great trees wrapped around with checkered cloth patterned in black and white, signifying "the opposites:" good and evil.

- In Burma, the Karen people still say that nature spirits inhabit very large trees and make themselves known by trembling their leaves even where there is no wind.

- Saving the worst 'til last to curdle your blood, an old German law forbade the peeling of a live tree's bark. Anybody caught in this sacrilege was cut open and his guts wrapped round and round the desecrated tree!

Pages and pages could be filled with stories of Druids, maypoles, charms, girls married to trees, trees slit lengthwise and pulled open to heal a child that would be passed through it. Without question, there has always been a powerful connection between humans and the trees that share our living space.

What pains we have taken to venerate our trees! We have always, always, always cared.

The soul when it comes to the leaping place,
encounters a tree called "Ulu-La-i-o-walu"
which forms the roadway into the other world.

Hawaiian myth

Every spirit builds itself a house;
and beyond its house a world;
and beyond its world a heaven.

Ralph Waldo Emerson, *Nature*

Zeus Lives

Above the sacred mountain, thunder booms and rumbles like the beating of great drums. It echoes over the hills, fertile fields, and out across the warm Aegean Sea. Lightning crackles from dark, roiling clouds and rain begins sweeping the dry earth.

Zeus, god of gods, still speaks through thunder and hurls lightning bolts at anyone who angers him. Upon this mountain was his dwelling place. For more than 2,200 years his mighty altar loomed on the mountain's brow. The place is Pergamum, Turkey.

A bolt of lightning crashes. "That was close, Zeus sounds irritated," I say to my companion as we struggle up a thousand footsteps on huge stone slabs to the ruins of this once great city. It rivaled Athens in glory and grandeur. We brace against the wind and pelting rain as our hurriedly bought pink child's umbrella collapses piteously against the gale. "Zeus is giving us the full effect."

At last, drenched and breathless, we reach the summit and stand gazing out upon the countryside spread below. Wind moans through the abandoned ruins.

Suddenly we catch our breath. Something living gleams bright against the dark sky. The silvery, storm-tossed branches of a little olive tree are wildly waving in the whistling wind. Clinging to and fluttering from every branch and leaf are hundreds and hundreds of white papers as high as hands can reach. The tree looks as if caught in a blizzard, bearing paper fruit instead of olives.

The rain eases. We watch as some travelers stop to write something on their own paper scraps, tying them carefully to the already crowded branches. They hurry off.

"What is going on here?" I say. "Could it be that people are still asking favors of Zeus and sending him their paper prayers even now?" A low roll of thunder fades to the south.

I picture Zeus's great temple altar as it was in antiquity: three stories high with two side wings and lifelike wall sculptures of gods fiercely battling Titans. A flight of wide steps leads to sheltered pillars topped with statues. But nothing of it remains here.

Some words from Shelley's "Ozymandias" come to mind:

". . . And on the pedestal these words appear:
'My name is Ozymandias, King of kings;
Look on my works, ye Mighty, and despair!'
Nothing beside remains. Round the decay
Of that colossal wreck, boundless and bare
The lone and level sands stretch far away."

I pause, transfixed as my mind reflects back across the centuries, envisioning all the people who have ever journeyed to this mountain temple. I can almost hear their voices on the wind and strain to listen. A ghostly vision begins forming in my imagination.

I see an old couple, wearing the simple tan-colored tunics of 2,000 years ago, his to the knees and hers to the ankles. They approach the mighty altar of Zeus with offerings, hoping to curry favor. She speaks from the past:

"It is Zeus! He comes, I hear his voice in the thunder!" says the woman.

"Ah, Father Zeus has answered my prayers!" says the man. "He sends rain to water my crops. Truly this is a place of power. How gracious is father Zeus."

"This gracious rain soaks my clothes," says the woman. "I needed not this much graciousness."

"Hush!" says the man. "We will be punished!"

"Zeus grants or punishes as he pleases," says the woman fatalistically. "Just my destiny to be punished after climbing a thousand steps burdened with this heavy tribute. For this I have cleansed and sacrificed?"

A loud thunderclap shakes the ground and echoes across the hills. Lightning flashes, an eagle screams from its high perch atop the shrine.

. . . some travelers stop to write something on their own paper scraps, tying them carefully to the already crowded branches.

"It is Zeus! He appears in the form of the eagle to warn us," says the man.

"Oh do not punish us great Zeus!" says the woman. "See, we bring gifts."

"Beg him more," whispers the man.

Rain cascades down the long, wide flight of altar steps and soaks their sandals as the two crouch in a muddy puddle awaiting their fate. Then the rain begins to ease. A gentle breeze moves the clouds away and sun peeps through. The eagle soars off into a rain-washed sky.

The man and woman get up off their knees, squeeze water from their sopping clothes, and clasping hands, gaze up at the sunlit altar. "How splendid it is, grandest in all the world," the man says. "Those gods and Titans look real enough to walk off the walls and down these very steps."

"Good thing old Zeus won," says the woman, "or we would be on our knees to those brutish Titans and crushed beneath their giant feet."

"Hush, in the name of Zeus!" says the man. "You will have them eating us for dinner as the Titan Kronos ate his children, spitting our bones into the salty sea! Do you want us cursed for all eternity?"

You will have them eating us for dinner as the Titan Kronos ate his children, spitting our bones into the salty sea! Do you want us cursed for all eternity?

The visions and voices fade away as the storm passes to the south. Sunlight now glints in puddles and glitters off the leaves of the olive tree, where the paper wishes hang dripping. Is that an eagle circling above?

We take a last look at the olive tree then turn to walk back down the mountain. Memories of what I imagined I saw and heard may fade. But that bright little olive tree will live in my memory forever.

But what of the invisible remnants, the psychic memory, captured in this place of power? Something stirs pilgrims here. The potency of old Zeus lingers and he still hurls thunder bolts, dispensing rewards or punishments. A flow of influence seems to rise up from the rocky soil. Haunting echoes remain of the rituals performed, and of prayer fragments chanted by all the humans who have ever worshiped and left offerings.

The little olive tree with its written petitions takes its turn now as a living agent of Zeus, receiving his prayers.

How do people know to do this petitioning? How do people from distant lands and cultures fall in stride so easily? There must be something in us eager to carry the past forward, a need for connection or continuity, perhaps. But no mistaking that it is quite real. Deep down we believe in prayers answered and wishes granted. Here is a place where people believe it could happen. People all over this world believe that magical sources can be tapped in certain holy places. Perhaps it excites some longing to connect with the strength and power of the old gods.

Zeus Lives

The skilled poet is one who knows much through natural gift, but those who have learned their art chatter turbulently, vainly against the divine bird of Zeus."

Pindar (518-438 BCE)

- There is another tree, also an olive, beside a lovely lake in Turkey. It is about five minutes' walk down a little path, off a main road between distant towns. The tree and an altar/tomb are decorated with trinkets and wrapped objects. In this case, it marks the grave of a venerated personage whose bones are thought to retain something of his essence and even the power of healing. The tree represents him. With its deep roots into the Underworld, receiver of our bones, and its high branches touching the heavens, this tree offers a living hope, and comfort.

- Pergamum, Turkey, was once the center of ancient civilization, rivaling Athens. The Temple of Zeus, a masterpiece of Hellenistic art with its richly carved marble friezes, was one of the wonders of the ancient world. It might still be there had it not been removed to Berlin, Germany, in the 1870s. It shares a fate with countless other fabulous works of art in museums far from their origins. This one was taken by consent of the ruling sultan. Some say it was pillage, some say preservation. Maybe it is both.

- In about 500 BCE, Esclepius, benevolent healer/god was revered at Pergamum and was connected with trees, herbs, and snakes. Somehow, the tradition of powerful healing has come down through the centuries, and so informed visitors "connect" here.

- Not far from Pergamum are the ruins of Assos, another mountain kingdom. Hermeias, its ruler (in 345 BCE.), had been a student of Plato. He brought Aristotle to live there and other philosophers, poets, mathematicians, scientists, physicians, and artists, to exchange ideas. The kingdom prospered; exciting ideas filled the air. Thugs, for its riches, destroyed it.

    How many glorious works of art have been destroyed? How many brilliant ideas lost or forgotten? How many times must we piece together the tattered fragments of magnificent civilizations?

Here is a place where people believe it could happen.

The Kauris of New Zealand

Tucked within the smooth green hills of New Zealand's North Island, not far from the surging Tasman Sea, lies a timeless virgin forest called Waipoua. Within its cool, shaded sanctuary rare treasures are protected, for here live the gigantic kauri pines. They are massive, with white "quilted" trunks. Not only are they among the largest and oldest living trees on our planet but they are also the last of their kind surviving on earth. And they grow only in New Zealand, in this small preserve.

It all began about 135 million years ago when New Zealand was once the lower right-hand corner of the supercontinent called Gondwanaland. Pretty soon a low, subterranean rumble began shaking the continent until a rift appeared, and slowly that corner started tearing away. With barely a lurch, New Zealand shoved off in a northeasterly direction across the blue Pacific Ocean on its unhurried voyage. There it settled down to live out its remaining existence in blissful isolation.

It is precisely because of this remoteness from outside influences that nearly all of the plants and animals found there are unique. They have evolved into unusual forms never seen on any other landmasses. Of all these rare species kauris are the most spectacular.

Most or us would recognize the towering redwoods and mammoth sequoias of California. But who among us except a proud New Zealander could describe a kauri or even know its name? Yet kauris are spectacular trees.

How big? Here's a true story to tweak your imagination: It seems there was a surveyor back in the late 1800s who, while tramping through New Zealand's vast, virgin forest, glimpsed from the corner of his eye, what looked like a cliff face. On closer inspection he was stunned to find that the "cliff" was actually an immense tree as wide and white as a house.

Surely, you scoff, anybody can tell a tree from a cliff. Yet once you discover that the tree's pale, stone-like trunk does not taper as it grows skyward but grows straight up for about a hundred and fifty feet before deciding to branch out you will see the source of the surveyor's forgiveable error in perception.

Here's another story about the biggest kauri on record. It grew in the mountains at the head of Tararu creek. They called it "the Kauri Ghost," because all that remained of it was its stump. But what a stump! It measured 28 feet across and 88 feet around. And, remember, its width held like a column for two-thirds of its entire height.

Now picture a very large museum room with a ceiling 28 feet high, on whose end wall is painted a footprint of "the Kauri Ghost" marking a circle from floor to ceiling. This tree, when turned on its side, would entirely fill the room and extend out to a length of at least 150 feet. BIG.

The high-spirited, beautifully tattooed, and deeply spiritual aboriginal Maoris of New Zealand have given noble names to their oldest kauris, names like *Tane Mahuta* ("god of the forest") and *Te Matua Nghere* ("father of the forest") names that honor and dignify these revered elders.

The Meeting

I barely slept the night before driving into the Waipoua forest to meet my first kauri. Dark, gloomy clouds shrouded the treetops, not the conditions I'd hoped for meeting the great Tane Mahuta. (Then, one cannot just order up perfection.) I clumped onto the raised, wood-plank path leading to the god of the forest, turning and turning again through the fern-filled primeval forest, knee deep in low-growing evergreen plants. Most of the trees I passed were other kinds, and of average size.

But what a stump! It measured 28 feet across and 88 feet around. And remember, its width held its girth, like a column for two thirds of its entire height.

It was quiet but for some birds hidden within the leafy canopy flutter–ing softly. Then the blue-wattled Kokako birds called their wonderfully entertaining flute-like musical phrases, just as their ancestors had been doing for countless generations of seemingly endless years gone by.

To the Maori people, this forest was revered as a sacred treasure store. Its flora and fauna were put there by Tane, the god of nature. It was Tane who taught them how to live and how to subsist from the forest.

As I thought about these things, walking the path that turned yet again, all at once it appeared! There it was, the great god of the forest, and at that very moment miraculously the sun burst forth, flooding the mighty white trunk with a shaft of brilliant light. Its skin shone brighter even than the pictures I'd seen on postcards. What a sight! This magnificent old kauri absolutely dwarfed every living thing around it. It made full-grown trees look like spindly adolescents.

Respectfully, I greeted the old tree, then stood head back, gazing in dreamy admiration and contemplative reverie. I searched my mind for some kind of perspective and comparison. The ancient coastal redwoods of California loom darkly skyward, and the gargantuan sequoias of the High Sierra mountains lord over their space like Old Testament prophets. The kauris in contrast are guileless, undaunting, even approachable and friendly. You get the feeling that you could strike up a congenial conversation: "So how have things been going for the past couple-thousand years? Any events stand out?"

I would have thrown myself at its feet, if not for a fence put there to protect its shallow roots from the likes of us. I scrutinized its great breadth, its height, and high branches, home to some staghorn ferns sprouting cozily up there. The kauri's skin was "quilted," with indentations in a diagonal pattern, adding a sort of homey familiarity to the scene, so sweet for one so old. Unassuming, uncompetitive, and unconcerned. How admirable.

The sun dimmed, the clouds merged in overcast again depriving the scene of some of its glamour. A woman passed by, irritatingly untouched by the presence of the great god of the forest, saying, "Well, that wasn't so much." I nearly challenged her to a fist fight right there on the spot. The very idea of saying something like that, and within earshot. But that was simply my humanness venting. Tree gods aren't petty.

To live so long and be so benign. As human thought goes, improbable.

My thoughts flashed back to what an Irish scholar had said about nature spirits gifting appreciators with sudden rays of sunshine. "That just

To the Maori people, this forest was revered as a sacred treasure store. Its flora and fauna were put there by Tane, the god of nature. It was Tane who taught them how to live and how to subsist from the forest.

The Kauris of New Zealand

happened to me!" I gave grateful thanks, feeling deeply blessed by the spirits' silent kindness.

Retracing my steps back down the turning path toward the road, I thought about the early Maoris who had no need of farms, for did not Tane provide them with fern root, birds and berries enough to sustain them without destroying their forest source? If they needed a tree felled to make a canoe, their priest would briefly lift "Tapu" restrictions (meaning something that is holy or sacred and treated with great respect) by reciting the proper incantations to Tane. So, also, were prayers and chants performed for the taking of any of Tane's "children," a bird or even a berry.

I thought of the paltry few kauris left and felt saddened.

The remaining Kauri giants are in their middle age now in the range of 2,000 years, merely half their life expectancy. If allowed to live out their natural lives, they will bring stunned awe to our descendants; that is, if people will just leave them alone and if we conduct ourselves as the caretakers we need to be in order to facilitate that future meeting. True, fires have claimed some along the way, but it is humans who have caused the greatest devastation since finding New Zealand, about 200 years ago.

Purpose

The 1800s were bad times for those old kauris, and for all their neighboring trees, for that matter. They were felled by the thousands for timber, or cleared to make way for farmland. Imagine, only 10 to 15 percent of the ancient forests remain today, and those few spared because they were inaccessible. But to be fair, preserves were set aside too, even though it was said that nobody was very sure exactly what for. Back then everything had to have a purpose, and what good was a purposeless forest?

So there went the kauris. Their beautiful, honey-colored wood, so straight and strong and easy to work, was made into everything from ship masts to tea trays. Everybody wanted some of it; and so nice, too, that the wood carried such a lovely, delicate, sweet scent.

Astoundingly, there have been 55,000-year-old kauris brought up from ancient bogs with wood as bright, beautiful, and easily worked as that of newly harvested trees.

But as desirable as their wood was, their very blood was precious. Kauris were bled for their marvelous, valuable resin from which a fast-drying varnish was made. In fact, globs of golden kauri amber (fossilized resin) big as human skulls were mined from the depths of the earth and swampy bogs. The "gum diggers" then melted it down. There is a room in the kauri museum in Matakohe with shelves filled with beautiful, translucent kauri amber, some with ancient bugs captured forever, in what they expected would be a short stopover but instead stayed for eternity.

Did I connect with a kauri spirit? Yes, in that bright, magic moment, I believe I did.

After Words

- The biggest and oldest trees on earth grow in California. Redwoods, sequoias, and bristlecone pines, like the sweet scented Polynesian kauri, are all conifers.

- Coastal redwoods of California, which live to 2,200 years, are the tallest trees, growing to 380 feet. They are more than 20 feet wide just above their swollen bases, but they taper as they rise. So, they don't look as huge as kauris. Giant sequoias reach a height of 300 feet, are more than 101 feet around, 30 feet wide at ground level, but taper to 27 feet. A stump was found to be 4,000 years old.

- The wizened, windblown bristlecone pines, though not big, reach a height of almost 50 feet and average more or less 5 feet around. Yet they can reach an age of over 5,000 years.

- Redwood roots are only 5 to 10 feet deep. The roots spread out an intricate network aided by fungi growing along the roots that supply nutrients from the soil. Groves of networking redwoods join together to support each other. Please protect them.

The Kauris of New Zealand

The Sacred Trees

The Bodhi Tree

Tree of Truth and Awakening

The amazing transformation of a prince named Siddhartha into one of the world's greatest spiritual leaders was accomplished with the aid of a fig tree. Siddhartha is now known as the Buddha, and the tree is now called the Bodhi, Bo (the Great Awakener, Tree of Truth). But that comes later . . . here's how the story began.

About 2,500 years ago in the far north of India in an area now called Nepal, there lived a proud king named Suddhodana. He ruled over a warrior cast called the Gautama clan. One night the king's wife, Maya, had a powerful dream of conceiving a baby, symbolized by a great white elephant, and that she would bear a son. A hermit seer came to announce that her son would either be a great king or a great holy man. This worried the king. He wanted his kingly lineage to continue through his son, which would not happen if his son became a holy man.

Following the custom of those days, Queen Maya journeyed to her father's kingdom to give birth, but had to stop early to give birth in a garden beneath a sal tree. She named the baby Siddhartha, meaning "he who achieves his aim." Queen Maya died a few days later.

The baby was cared for by one of Maya's relatives in the king's palace. He was given every possible luxury and indulgence so that he would not turn toward a religious life. And the king carefully shielded Siddhartha from religious teachings, nor had he knowledge of suffering beyond the palace walls. Siddhartha's upbringing was martial and rigorous, as was expected of a ruling aristocrat. He excelled at horseback riding, chariot driving, javelin throwing, and shooting arrows. He grew quite tall and strong and was proud of his accomplishments. He learned to write and had an excellent, clever mind; yet his disposition was serious and contemplative.

He was married at age 16 or 17 to a cousin named Yasodhara and eventually fathered a son named Rahula. But by the time Siddhartha reached the age of 29 he was bored with pampering and dissatisfied with his guarded, protected life. He now questioned everything and wanted to see the outside world.

So he arranged for his departure, and turning his back on kin and court, fled off with his chariot driver into the unfamiliar world beyond palace walls. His adventure of discovery turned into a very long and hard journey. He was horrified to see a very old man, then a diseased man, and a decaying corpse. But he also saw a calm, holy hermit. Siddhartha was learning, and determined to experience all he could. He saw suffering of every kind, poverty, avarice, degradation, and desolation of soul.

In despair he wondered if there were some way to escape the tragic frailties of the human condition. Then he remembered the calm holy hermit with his begging bowl. Renouncing his life of privilege, he became a hermit. As he wandered, he found three teachers and, following their examples, gave away all his belongings, even his clothes. Naked, carrying only an alms bowl, he entered into a life of severe discipline, fasting, and meditation. This way he lived for six years, wasting to skin and bones. Yet though he gained self-discipline, he found neither inner peace nor spiritual enlightenment.

Surely, he thought, achieving enlightenment is not meant to be so difficult; there must be a middle way toward harmony with all-that-is, to be free and one with the ultimate Source. That thought was to change his life forever. (It would also change the lives of millions who would one day follow his example and wise teachings.)

Siddhartha was now 35 years old. Unwavering in his quest for enlightenment, he went to the great pipal fig tree in Bodh Gaya (now in India) and sat himself down against a depression in its mighty trunk to ponder. Then he vowed: "Though my bones waste away and my blood dries up, I shall not leave this tree until I have broken through to

He now questioned everything and wanted to see the outside world.

the Truth." He went into deep meditation sheltered beneath the tree's massive branches, sustained by its strength. A huge *naga*, serpent spirit, came to watch over him.

There began what has been called his 49-day vigil under the sacred tree. And during all that time, he sat firm and fixed. His body, mind, and soul struggled against upheavals, trials, tribulations, and temptations of every kind, challenging and shaking the foundations of his very being. Yet he remained unmoved. He affixed himself to the immovable center of the universe, as though to the still hub of a wheel whose outer spokes spin, or to the calm at the center of a whirling wind.

Then a brilliant light enveloped him. Wondrously, all barriers melted away as he transformed the assaults upon him into beautiful flowers. He saw Truth at last!

In this high state of exaltation he seemed to climb the Cosmic Tree where from its top he could see everything everywhere. No longer was he subject to the conditions and limitations of the physical world. He was free! The prince Siddhartha had become the Buddha: the Enlightened One.

He was given the vision of an eight-spoked wheel, symbol of the Noble Eightfold Path that would help anyone who quested towards enlightenment.

The compassionate and charismatic Buddha lived 80 years, traveling and gathering eager followers of all kinds, and teaching the Middle Way to those who also longed to free themselves from the attachments to worldly things and cease the pain of human existence. He died, as he had been born, lying between two trees.

Now here is an important twist often overlooked. In the earliest Buddhist texts it is the Bodhi, Bo tree, not the Buddha, that is referred to as the Great Awakener. In early sculptures the tree was always portrayed without Buddha to show that he had freed himself from all earthly attachments and had risen beyond this plane.

The great tree also represents the process of enlightenment, since it draws nourishment from the sun above and sustenance from the earth below, sending sap rising through its trunk to the topmost branches at its crown. This is similar to the actual physical process of enlightenment, where a very fine *kundalini,* life-force energy, travels up the spine to the brain, delivering the wonderful, transforming light.

The tree, then, is an image we can easily understand. The subtle energies needed for spiritual transformation become awakened at the

He was given the vision of an eight-spoked wheel, symbol of the Noble Eightfold Path that would help anyone who quested towards enlightenment.

root *chakra,* or energy center, at the base of the spine. As the energy rises up the spine, it activates all seven *chakras* on the way toward the goal at the top of the head. This energy bursts open "the thousand-petaled lotus" where enlightenment is experienced.

After Words

❧ The Noble Eightfold Path:
right understanding,
right view,
right thought,
right speech,
right action,
right livelihood,
right effort,
right concentration.

❧ The Four Noble Truths: (1) Suffering is inherent in existence. (2) Ignorance is the origin of suffering, due to attachment and craving. (3) Attachment and craving can be stopped. (4) The way to stop attachment and craving is to follow the Eightfold Path, thereby ending suffering.

❧ Some notables living on earth around Buddha's lifetime: Lao Tzu and Confucius in China; Ezekiel in Israel; Pythagoras in Greece; Zarathustra in Persia.

❧ The Bo tree was a pipal fig tree, *Ficus religiosa,* a large, long-lived species.

❧ In Bodh Gaya, India, a pipal fig tree reported to have come from a cutting of the original Bodhi tree, still grows there and is venerated.

❧ In another village in India there exists a temple within a large banyan tree with a door in its trunk, stairs leading up to it, and an arched frame around the door. Devotees hand-water it.

❧ There are at least 500 million Buddhist devotees in the world today.

❧ The sixth century BCE was a time of religious and political turmoil and brutality. Traditional religious values were questioned by thoughtful minds searching for life's meaning. Many new teachers emerged with insights into the nature of man and existence.

❧ Buddha said there was no mediator between mankind and the divine; that one must test and find one's own truth, not just blindly follow another's.

❧ Buddha often taught within groves of trees.

Before enlightenment, chopping wood and carrying water,
After enlightenment, chopping wood and carrying water.
But oh, the difference

Traditional Buddhist saying

Tree of the Norse

Yggdrasil

Long ago when time was new
space was somewhat calm,
Then a Frost Giant crawled
from a crack in space
And stupidly looked around.

Seeing nothing and hearing nothing,
he bellowed a terrible shout.
Hurling fire and ice,
made a mess of space,
What a loathsome, despicable lout.

This oaf's name was Ymir (ee-mer), who was chaos itself. Pretty soon a god named Odin came striding along, composing rhymes. Odin was a thinking sort of fellow and on a quest for knowledge. Though Odin knew many things and could do many things, he was never satisfied. Earnestly, he thirsted to know more. But his search was

Then dirt and rocks heaved up and with an earsplitting blast a gigantic ash tree burst through. The tree grew so fast and huge that the universe and all nine realms were sheltered within its mighty spread.

endlessly interrupted by the chaos caused by Ymir. No sooner did Odin find a thing than Ymir broke it.

Finally Odin got so fed up with the constant turmoil caused by Ymir, he said to his two brother gods, "Enough of this chaos! There will be no order until the oaf is gone, and that Ymir is chaos itself!" So they killed Ymir.

Sure enough, things calmed down. Order began arranging itself into place in an amazing way, helped by Odin and his brothers, of course.

For out of Ymir's body they molded the universe. From his blood flowed the seas. From his bones piled the mountains. From his skull burst forth the heavens and from his brains floated the clouds.

Yggdrasil

Suddenly a great trembling shook the earth. A loud rumbling came from deep below. Then dirt and rocks heaved up and with an earsplitting blast a gigantic ash tree burst through. The tree grew so fast and huge that the universe and all nine realms were sheltered within its mighty spread. The name of this tree was Yggdrasil (ig-dra-sil), known as the Tree of Knowledge.

But the keys to this knowledge were hidden away in symbols, pictures, and stories. The symbols were in, on, under, and around Yggdrasil. The tree held the secrets of Time, Space, and Destiny.

But secrets must be kept safe, lest any careless oaf misuse them. For there is power in knowledge. And knowledge without wisdom is dangerous.

Odin longed to know of destiny and what fate had in store. If only he understood the secret language of symbols, he could decode Yggdrasil, and gain knowledge, wisdom, and discover his destiny.

Sybil

So Odin awakened Sybil, the soothsayer, deeply sleeping in the shade of the great tree. She frowned darkly, cross at being aroused from her trance. But Odin, being a god, commanded: "Tell me of destiny." Sybil lifted an eyebrow, gave Odin a wry smile and teased him, saying, "I will give clues to those who are worthy." But Odin would not be put off. Again he said, "Tell me of destiny!"

At last she gave in, and squinting into the future, she said, "Beware! The end of the world, called Ragnarok, will be the doom of the gods." This sounded pretty serious. What did this mean?

Then, turning her head, Sybil looked into the past and said:

"I remember the giants who gave me birth.
  I know of nine worlds entered through the Tree of Knowledge.
  The tree is wet with waters white.
  The dews of this water fall into the dales.
  The tree grows ever green by Earth's well."

After saying these mysterious words she fell back into a dead sleep.

Odin pondered and puzzled over Sybil's words, then said to himself, "Could the white water be Mimer's forbidden Spring of Wisdom and Remembrance? Then I shall drink of it. Did she not say that I will find it at Earth's well by the green tree Yggdrasil?"

Quickly, Odin went in search of the god Mimer and found him sitting by his milky spring. Odin gathered himself, bowed nobly to a fellow god, and asked casually, "Might I drink from your spring?"

Mimer narrowed his eyes, answering slowly, "Yes, you may drink. But first give one of your eyes as a sacrifice if you would have the waters of wisdom."

Odin wanted wisdom and knowledge so much that he willingly plucked out an eye and threw it into the well waters of wisdom.

Then he strode to the well's edge and drank deeply from the forbidden waters. Immediately, visions appeared. In these visions he saw the language of symbols. "Ah, so this is their meaning!" said Odin. "I must save this language." So he carved it into twenty-four magic rune stones to use as an alphabet to write down letters into words. Now, what before was only spoken aloud, could be read. Odin now understood and could put meaning to the symbols in, on, under, and around the tree.

"My journey to knowledge, wisdom, and destiny is quickening with Yggdrasil as my steed; for it is said, 'to shorten a journey, ride a fast horse.'" Odin laughed, slapped his thigh, and shouted "Yggdrasil, Steed of Odin!"

At that an eight-legged horse named Sleipner came galloping by. Odin leapt upon his sturdy back and rode onto the magical path toward his destiny. Two ravens flew with Odin as he faithfully followed the path through hills and dales, gathering warriors in the halls of Valhalla for the final battle that would happen at Ragnarok according to Sybil's prophecy.

Tree of the Norse

"Skree"

One day as Odin sat meditating, a great thought came to him: "To be free of the chains that bind us with trials and strife, all we must do is rise above the muck of it!" All at once, with the sound of a breaking chain, his shape shifted into that of a magical eagle. Flapping his mighty wings, he leapt into the sky and soared beyond the stars. At last he could travel freely through the spirit world and learn its secrets.

Finally the eagle circled down and around, coming to rest atop Yggdrasil, on a branch called Peace Giver.

The moment he touched the branch, a falcon named Vedfalnir fluttered gently down upon the eagle's head, settling carefully between the eagle's eyes. The sharp-eyed falcon thus functioned as a magical third eye. With this far sight it could see everything in the universe, even into all nine worlds.

Odin could now change his shape when it suited him. But because Odin was so linked with earth and humans, he heroically made one last sacrifice. And so he did a shocking and mysterious thing. He hung himself on Yggdrasil for nine days and nine nights! Then a thunderous "Clang!" resounded as the final, invisible chain shattered. This is how Odin overcame the world.

And this is how he discovered the greatest mystery of all:

The world is an illusion, a fantasy dreamed into being in the beginning!

"That's what it's all about? Why, that means that we can dream whatever we will, and, believing, it will be true!" Odin then drew in a deep breath, threw back his head, and laughed so hard that tears poured down his ruddy Norse cheeks. His wild laughter filled the universe. And if you listen closely you might still hear Odin's laughter echoing through space.

Ragnarok

Sybil had told Odin that the world would end at Ragnarok. The great tree Yggdrasil would tremble and shake and everything, including the gods, would come tumbling down, a gloomy end, indeed. Of course, those who learned to fly free in the universe could escape (yet, alas, not Odin who was eaten by the giant wolf, Fenrir. Such are the things that happen in the world of matter).

But wait! This is not really the final ending because from the trunk of the tree will come a man and a woman. They will create a new race

of people. They will bring amazing ideas into their world to renew and replenish it!

And then what? It all begins again, like a repeating round song, yet each time the tone is a little higher. Each new beginning brings a chance to become wiser! So, as the round song suggests:

Row, row, row your boat, gently down the stream,
and go merrily, for life is but a dream!

Unraveling Some Symbols of Yggdrasil

- In the beginning, All-Father created Fire and Ice. When hot flames clashed with cold ice, they exploded. Bam! The ice melted into the great crack in space called Ginnungagap. It melted into a Frost Giant called Ymir, symbol of chaos.

- Order could only happen when chaos was gone.

- The tree is the hub or axis of the universe that connects all nine worlds.

- Though it does not seem so, the universe is in perfect order, from the tiniest germ to the mightiest giants of space.

- The lowest plane is the restless Underworld, in the roots below ground.

- The middle plane is Middle Earth, at the trunk where people live. It was formed from Ymir's eyebrows.

- The highest plane is Asgaard, in the crown of the tree. This is the Heavenly Realm: land of the gods.

- From Yggdrasil's trunk came an ash tree and an alder tree that became the first man and the first woman: Asker and Embla.

- A chattering squirrel named Ratatosk scurries about spreading gossip, insults, and discord. It is unwise to listen to him.

- In the Underworld, three great roots each seek nourishing springs:
  The first root goes to the land of the dead called Hel.
  The second root goes to the kingdom of the old Frost Giants.
  The third root goes to the gods of Judgment, who daily resolve disputes as they sit by the Fountain of Fate, also called Urdar's spring.

- The rainbow Bifrost Bridge is a guarded road to the Heavenly Realms.

- Three wise goddesses of Fate faithfully pour life-giving water from the Fountain of Fate and Wisdom onto the tree's roots, and on the Seeds

Tree of the Norse

of Possibilities. They take turns weaving an intricate pattern from the strands of human fate.

- Four deer, named: Dain, Duney, Durathror, and Dvalin, are North, South, East, and West. They devour the tree's leaves that never wither.

- A snake called Niogghr endlessly gnaws at the roots to destroy them, hence, the tree, and the gods, too. He is helped by millions of worms.

- But the wise, patient goddesses see what is happening. They weave and mend the world back together as the snake chews it up.

- Yet there is hope, for lying quietly in the soil are the Seeds of Promise. The seeds are waiting their chance to sprout.

- In the vast sea around the tree swims a snake, his tail is in his mouth. This symbolizes the endless circle of life and eternity.

It is said that the Yggdrasil tree myth is the single most important myth using a tree as its central focus.

After Words

- ❦ It is said that the Yggdrasil tree myth is the single most important myth using a tree as its central focus. My interpretation incorporates parts from all of the Yggdrasil stories I could find, being true to the gist while clarifying its loose ends. Since no doctrine is involved, I humbly take poetic license.

- ❦ The Indo-European, Greek gods, heroes of Troy, the Egyptian, Assyrian, Buddhist, and Christian stories have influenced the Yggdrasil myth.

- ❦ The Hindu word *maya* in its varying degrees means the "illusion of life."

- ❦ Hindus regarded the grand universe as a divine tree, grown from a single seed sown in space.

- ❦ The fast, eight-legged horse could be a metaphor related to Buddha's Eightfold Path to enlightenment. Odin's sacrifice on the tree is an allusion to Christ's sacrifice on the cross, added by Christian interpreters.

- ❦ Zeus made the third race of men from ash trees.

- ❦ Fatalism runs deep in Norse stories. (Did you notice?)

Tree of Knowledge

An imagined conversation between Eve and the Serpent, before The Fall…

It was that glorious harvest time of year when the apples were red, ripe and delicious, and the air tinted soft gold, with sunlight gilding every leaf. Eve, a very young woman then, came strolling through the autumn afternoon, tenderly touching this or that plant, plucking berries, and tossing them to the little creatures always tagging along: this day, a lamb, and an antelope with a dove riding his antlers. Life was simple and life was sweet in the beautiful Garden of Eden. Here, there was no need for clothing.

Presently Eve came to a place where the path circled wide around the mighty Tree of Knowledge. Eve lingered to admire its luxuriant splendor, its bounty of bright, beautiful apples hanging heavy on its branches, their pungent fragrance all the more enticing her desire for the smallest taste. Alas, this was the forbidden fruit the Lord-God had warned Adam not to eat, even before Eve was created.

Just then a branch rustled and a snake's head appeared, swaying back and forth. In a dry, whispery voice Snake called down to her, "Good afternoon Eve. Come closer, so that we might converse."

"Hello," said Eve, who had never before noticed the gleaming, sinuous creature living in the Tree of Knowledge.

Snake slithered nearer, whispering, "I see you desire this tasty fruit. It is like no other. Come, have a bite. Your eyes will be opened, and you will

Snake slithered nearer
and whispered, "I see you
desire this tasty fruit.
 It is like no other, come,
have a bite."

become like the gods, knowing good and evil. Wouldn't that be nice?" Snake's eyes narrowed shrewdly.

"No I mustn't," said Eve, remembering what Adam had told her about God's warning. But curious as one so new to the world would be, she stepped closer and asked, "What is your name, please?"

Snake stretched, hissed impressively, extending his two-tipped-tongue, replying mysteriously, "I have many names in many lands. Here, I am called Guardian of the Tree of Knowledge. But you can call me Snake."

"And what are your other names, if I may ask?" said Eve.

Then rising majestically and swaying hypnotically back and forth, Snake began to intone:

"I am the great serpent from ancient and future times, feared, adored and worshipped on every continent." He spoke slowly, savoring every word.

"I am Sky-Serpent who formed the Milky Way; and Life giver, with my copper body and rising head of gold. I am the gigantic Snake, covering sun, moon and stars; and, I am very wise."

Eve, in rapt attention, began swaying with Snake as he droned on.

"I am Renewal, for by shedding my old worn skin, I can renew my body.

I am Ourobouros, with tail in my mouth showing the eternally repeating cycles.

I am the healer-snake on the physician's caduceus.

As Apep, the serpent-god from the night sky, I create chaos. As Da, Rainbow Serpent, I put the world in order. As serpent of light and serpent of darkness, I represent opposites."

Eve was becoming enchanted, seduced by Snake's marvelous words while Snake continued his hypnotic litany:

"I am the serpent of divine fire, kundalini energy, coiled at the base of the spine. I climb to the head, delivering enlightenment.

I am Guardian of truth and sacred places. I am Naga, protector of wells, rivers and springs."

Then with hushed solemnity and trembling with importance, Snake said at last, "I am the serpent of Knowledge and Wisdom, the whispering mind of individual consciousness and free will." Pausing for effect, but getting none, Snake said, "Well, Eve, what did you think of that?"

Eve was so impressed she could not speak. Her head was swimming with all those magnificent new words.

"Ah," said Snake lightly, speaking now as with a child, measuring Eve's sweet innocence, "Want to see me shift my shape and turn colors?"

Eve was quite overwhelmed, and declined his demonstration. Yet, more than anything, she wanted to understand those thrilling, marvelous words.

Then, recovering, she asked, "Snake, if I eat an apple, will I know as much as you?"

"Why Yesss, child," replied Snake soothingly. "All in due time, of course, and in your own way," he said with a cunning smile. "And, you will surely not die. Here, help yourself, take two."

Meanwhile, Adam was busy naming the endless supply of all earthly creatures that the Lord-God had said should be his assigned task on Earth.

Eve danced in, saying excitedly, "Here, Adam, I brought you a present. It's pretty, tastes good, and it will make you know very much."

"Great!" said Adam, "I'm hungry as a lion," ready for a time-out from his mind straining task, and a bite of what would make him know very much.

So Adam and Eve sat themselves down in the grass to eat their apples. But no sooner had their tongues touched the scarlet skin, than a flash of lightning and a crash of thunder shook the earth. In an instant everything changed forever more.

Well, as we all know, things just went from bad to worse. Their pure, childlike innocence had changed to guilt, just by tasting the fruit of the forbidden tree that introduced them to the knowledge of good and evil. So, in shame, they covered themselves with leaves, hiding from the Lord-God, who then banished them from the Garden where time did not exist, and thrust them amongst the thorns and thistles.

Thus began their long exile and punishment. Adam was evermore cursed to work by the sweat of his brow. Eve was evermore cursed to endure pain in childbirth, and Snake, slithering after them, was evermore cursed to endure their enmity.

But, some far off day, at the end of their long, uphill climb from childhood to maturity, exercising their newly found free will, experiencing torments, but also discovering joy, they would gain knowledge. They would learn good judgment and increase their wisdom. Through wisdom, they might understand the meaning of life. Knowing the meaning of life, they could at last release themselves from earthly attachments and reach the ultimate goal: union with the Creator. Will they? Will we?

After Words

❧ The Master advised that if we look inward, we would eventually find our way back to the Garden of Heaven, which, after all, is within.

Tree of Knowledge

Qabalah: Tree of Life

Tradition of the Children of Abraham

Back in the days when I was casting about for answers to the Big Questions, I came upon the Qabalah and was immediately intrigued. Here is a philosophic system cleverly arranged as a tree. Who could resist? There is something utterly irresistible about formulas that promise to reveal the secrets of the universe. Using Qabalah's methods, a person could get those answers to the questions we all know so well: Where did we come from? Where are we going? What's life all about? Why . . . ? Studying Qabalah's system promises to improve and empower our lives and to bring us deep, spiritual awakening. Qabalah (*Kaballah, Cabala*, literally, "tradition") is the mystical interpretation of the Old Testament.

Tradition says Qabalah was given to Adam in the beginning, then was passed down to Abraham, who passed it to certain unknown saints, who passed it to mysterious masters, who kept its light burning so that it can still be practiced today.

Qabalah stands at the very foundation of the Hebrew, Christian, and Islamic religions. But it has been kept secret, until recently.

"One is filled with admiration . . . at seeing a doctrine so logical, so simple and at the same time, so absolute . . . simple as the alphabet . . .

Don't throw pearls before swine [pigs], lest they trample them.

(Mathew 7:6)

a theology summed up by counting on one's fingers, profundity held within the hollow of an infant's hand," said scholar Albert Pike.

Even so, when I studied Qabalah, those many years ago, it was definitely *not* simple. It was *hard* and complicated because of all the padlocks protecting its golden secrets. I lost patience, asking in frustration, "What good are pearls of wisdom to us if they are locked in armored boxes?"

The caution, "Don't throw pearls before swine [pigs], lest they trample them" (*Mathew* 7:6) is worth remembering here. Such power must be kept safe from those who would surely abuse and misuse it.

However, things are changing. Qabalah is of such immense value in these troubled times that the old defenses, deliberate false walls, and blind alleys are being carefully removed for the sake of humanity. It is becoming accessible.

Qabalah is so vast in scope, however, that time is required to soak it in. It is worth the effort.

We begin. Starting with a simple diagram invitingly called the Tree of Life, it is actually a treasure map. The seeker follows special paths on a life-changing journey. Irresistible. This is my shortcut to envisioning it.

There are ten spheres (called, collectively, *sephiroth*) nicely organized on the tree. They are set in three orderly columns. Twenty-two "paths" connect them. The diagram looks a little like a board game, the object being to move from one sphere to the next to understand what part of life's experience it represents. We can stay as long as we like to explore a sphere's contents. Each sphere is unique. By examining our experiences while "in" a sphere (or realm of consciousness) and studying its connections or "correspondences," to things of like manner, we find a pearl of wisdom to keep.

We might think of it visually: When all ten spheres have been mined of their pearls, and understood, the tree lights up with the light of our understanding. We then become enlightened and are entitled to all the splendors promised.

If you've ever played hopscotch, you've participated in a sort of child's version of the Tree of Life, jumping from lower to higher numbers chalked on a sidewalk. It's a game of life that leads to "sky blue" or God: a ladder to heaven.

The spheres represent the original emanation of light from God, cast forth in the Beginning, and split up into ten parts. God's purpose, says Qabalah, was to create opportunities for us to experience all the things in

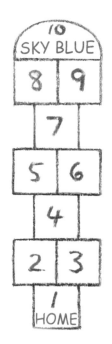

life necessary for an individual to learn and grow. When we successfully maneuver through these experiences, we will achieve the ultimate goal: the bliss of attaining union with God, one more soul returned to God. This is a cause for rejoicing in heaven and earth, the chiming of bells, the cheering of angels.

When this "graduation" happens, God mysteriously expands, if you can imagine "All" becoming "More." Not only do we need God, but God needs us as well. This business of an expanding God gives us purpose as co-creators in the whole process. We find ourselves responsible for giving the God-of-All-Creation assistance.

Our task is to combine all those separate emanations of light from God and soak them into ourselves so that we become whole. The tree diagram provides a frame of reference for all life's possible experiences. Each rung of the ladder is an experience on the trip up to the "Crown" or God.

By studying each sphere, learning its signs, symbols, colors, influences, designations, and so on, one eventually gains knowledge and understanding. This knowledge must be gained through our own efforts. And the questions we ask must be self-answered (you knew there was a catch).

It is remarkable, though, that help is never far away. Teachers will become available when we are ready for them. I know that the saying, "When the student is ready, the teacher appears" is a fact—from the following firsthand experience.

Shortly after I moved to San Francisco, I received a call out of the blue from a mysterious teacher of metaphysics, inviting me to study with him. After adjusting to the magical nature of the call, I agreed. Among other subjects, he knew Qabalah well. I listened carefully and learned to pronounce the unpronounceable names. I could see the fire of truth blazing within Qabalah. Although it seemed just out of reach, I got occasional flashes of insight anyway. There was indeed wisdom to be found.

But the process, back then, was diabolically complicated. Glancing around at my bright fellow students, I could almost see crackling sparks snapping from their brains, feel the heat of their laser-fast comprehension. At long last, a light dawned on me: Qabalah was a path made to order for brilliant intellectuals with mystical inclinations. So noted, feeling rather defeated and not ready, I bowed to the great Qabalah for what I had managed to absorb and tiptoed away.

Life is a succession of lessons, which must be lived to be understood.
Ralph Waldo Emerson.

When the student is ready the teacher appears.

Years passed, and another strange, wonderful thing happened after I decided to include Qabalah in this book. I probed my memory, got out the old books and wrote what I knew, but felt I must also find recent information to do it justice.

Where to start? My search was seemingly interrupted by a trip to New York City, where I found, to my astonishment, that our randomly chosen hotel in mid-Manhattan was located directly across from an elegant new place called Kabbalah Centre. I hurried over to make inquiries of any possible changes in the teachings. I attended a lecture and bought a book. Reassuringly, the ancient tradition has stayed intact, but now fresh breezes move through it removing the intentional blocks. Different teachers with new stories now invite the world in with open arms.

To those who have the right stuff, there is value in abundance to be found, and the secrets of the alchemists, who would change leaden souls to purest gold.

After Words

- The Tree of Life is sometimes shown upside down with its roots in heaven, its branches on earth. "As above, so below" is a phrase often repeated in Qabalah. There are still vast mysteries for the seeker to discover.

- This drawing is of the Hebrew Triad. Trinity of the first three spheres: The top is the crown; the other two represent the Father and the Mother. The three flame-like points represent this creative triad.

- The meanings of the ten spheres remain the same in both the Western Hermetic system and in the Hebrew system, differing only in interpretation.

- The names of the spheres vary, since one word can't fully describe all that a sphere contains. They derive from Hebrew words.

- The spheres, numbered in descending order, (looking like the zigzag of a lightning bolt) are: 1 Crown, 2 Wisdom, 3 Understanding, 4 Mercy, 5 Severity, 6 Beauty, 7 Victory, 8 Glory or Intelligence, 9 Foundation, 10 Kingdom.

- The spheres are arranged in three columns, each column designated a name: Mercy, on the right, Severity, on the left, and Mildness in the middle. The middle path, though slower, is the surest path to the Godhead.

    Godspeed.

The name of this infinite and inexhaustible depth
and ground of all being is God.

Paul Tillich (1886–1965)

Chocolate: Food of the Gods

Yes!

If I had a sacred tree it would be chocolate, of course; so just for fun I checked it out. What do you know! Chocolate *is* a sacred tree! I knew it.

The Olmecs, Mayans, Aztecs, and Toltecs of Mesoamerica who lived along and below the Gulf Coast of southern Mexico, were on to it right from the start. These people had fabulous cultures with heart-stopping myths, and breathtaking carvings, paintings, pottery, and poetry. They were the astronomers who invented an extremely accurate calendar. And, they loved their chocolate.

It all began about 3,600 years ago with the mysterious Olmecs, who had a high civilization, built pyramids, and flourished in the hot, humid, lowland forests of Mesoamerica. They are the same people who carved those colossal basalt heads, high as a man; but no one knows why. Little remains of their language except for sherds here and there, because the climate was so relentlessly unforgiving to perishable materials. They grew chocolate: *cacao* (ca-cow'). They called it, *ka ka'wa*.

Good news: Science has now proven that a flavonol (epicatechin) from certain cacao compounds is beneficial to the heart. It reduces the risk of blood clots, and improves circulation. So rejoice! Have one guiltless piece of dark chocolate a day. A grateful world thanks science.

I shall call it chocolate, so as not to confuse it with coca (cocaine), coco palm, or a species of starchy root called coco, or a common bean, also called coco. Besides, I like calling it a chocolate tree.

Way back then, only the elite were privileged to drink chocolate, the kings, nobles, warriors, and also traveling merchants, their delivery service. There is a connection between blood and chocolate: The red liquid running from the crushed seeds reminded the later Mayans and Aztecs (a bloody lot) of their precious blood, sacrifice, and death; so chocolate was important in their religious ceremonies. (Here, the bandied modern phrase, "I'd kill for a piece of chocolate," though innocently uttered, takes on a creepy meaning.)

The Mayans were a fatalistic people, stern but temperate, especially their well educated priests who were held to high standards and were expected to be chaste. Their philosophy was dualistic—good and evil determined the course of their lives—so they saw irony in the grim play of opposites in life. Later, deplorably, Cortez and the Spanish conquistadores (also a bloody lot) would toss all the Mayan writings they found into the bonfires of the Inquisition. Yet three priceless books were miraculously saved: written, and illustrated by their elevated, literate artist-scribes, with pictures of gods and texts telling that chocolate was their food.

The Rage for Chocolate

Ironically it is through the Spanish, in the early 1600s that Europeans learned about chocolate. Europeans didn't take to it at first. The watery drink was laced with chili pepper and spice, giving it what has been called by its appreciators a "pleasurable burn." Sugar is what made all the difference to the Europeans. Chocolate became the rage and everybody was thoroughly hooked. For instance, a noblewoman is teased to choose: "the love letter or your afternoon chocolate?"

The first known picture of chocolate being processed was painted on a beautiful Mayan pot in 750 CE. A woman is shown pouring a potion into a vessel from a height, so as to mix the fat part with the chocolate part, creating foam. To the Aztecs and Mayans this foam was happiness itself.

Sometimes they drank it hot, sometimes cold. Sometimes they mixed it with maize (corn, the staff of life), other times, with vanilla. Each drink was made in a specially shaped bowl designed for enhancing its flavor. Those recipes are the basis for the chocolate still drunk today in the Yucatan by Mayan descendents.

Finicky

The wonder, however, is that the now unstoppable worldwide chocolate craze ever began in the first place, since it all depends on such a fussy, finicky plant.

Chocolate is extremely hard to grow. It is prone to diseases and easily overcome by the least little night chill. It simply will not bear fruit outside of a narrow geologic band, 20 degrees north and 20 degrees south of the equator, nor at altitudes with temperatures below 60 degrees. It demands year around moisture or it despairs, gives up, and drops all of its evergreen leaves.

It is susceptible to "pod rots," "wilts" and growths called "witch's brooms." It detests wind, and its seeds won't sprout to make new plants unless kept in constant warmth and moisture. Then there are rats, squirrels, and monkeys, who steal the pods for the sweet, white, gelatinous pulp around the seeds, leaving the pits behind, which are bitter. So why on earth did we ever want to eat the seed pits? It involves a " precious thing," which I'll explain in a minute.

But, first, here are things to know about chocolate trees: The chocolate tree stands about 35 feet high; it is slender with drooping, oval, leathery leaves. Its ridged, warty pods range in color from yellow-orange to purple and pop directly out of its trunk and main branches. The pods begin as little star-shaped, cream-colored flowers. But, get this, the *only* way they can be pollinated is by really tiny gnat-like midges. So, no midges; no chocolate.

The wonder, however, is that the now unstoppable worldwide chocolate craze ever began in the first place, since it all depends on such a fussy, finicky plant.

The Precious Thing

The tough pods cannot be opened other than by animals or humans or by rot. There are 30 to 40 almond-shaped beans to a pod, and the beans, my dears, contain what the Aztecs called the "precious thing!" The precious thing, when chocolate is analyzed, consists of the things we humans naturally crave: caffeine, a stimulant and brain enhancer; serotonin, a mood-lifting hormone and stimulant; theobromine, likewise; and phenyl ethylamine, also a mood changing brain chemical. Together they are tonic or strengthening, antidepressive and antistress agents.

It "enhances pleasurable activities, including making love," says Dr. Herve Robert, who wrote a book in defense of chocolate. Chocolate is a reliable euphoric. And, as one passionate devotee winks and says, "Sex is merely a substitute for chocolate." Well bring on the chocolate!

Chocolate: Food of the Gods

Chocolate Money

When Cortez conquered Mexico in 1521, he found huge, royal store-houses filled with *cacao* beans that were used not only as food and drink but also as real currency to exchange for goods and to pay for labor.

An avocado was worth three cacao beans. One good turkey hen was worth 100 full cacao beans or 120 shrunken beans. Chocolate (okay, *cacao*) beans had the advantage of being easily carried, and if you got desperate, you could always eat them, with a little processing, of course. Chocolate contains carbohydrates, so it helps fight fatigue. Traveling soldiers ate them for this reason.

Grasp the enormity of chocolate's importance with this fact: Counterfeiters, those ever-ingenious forgers, actually made fake beans from chiseled avocado seeds—a little wax, a little clay, wrap them in a hull, and there you have it, fake money. Fake, lovingly carved, clay chocolate beans have been found in building sites, probably having served as symbolic offerings. The clay replicas were practical for their longevity, since the actual beans were too valuable to waste.

The World Tree

The Aztec World Tree mandala was designed as a diagram of the universe. It shows *chocolate* in the south quadrant: the south World Tree, adorned with a macaw bird, a large parrot with long tail and brilliant plumage, signifying its southern origin. It is associated with the color red for blood (blood and chocolate, both have red liquids.) There we have it: a sacred tree!

The god, or deity, of chocolate, or its tree spirit, perhaps, is shown as a stocky fellow, naked except for belt, necklace, and bracelets of beads made from jade or *cacao* beans. He wears a jaunty feathered hat and points to a fancy urn containing chocolate, and he sprouts big pods from feet to shoulders.

Nowadays, fine chocolate-makers are called chocolatiers.

I imagine the happy cry of chocolate lovers, "There go the three chocolatiers, their capes flying, spoons raised, making the world safe for chocolate!"

❧ Mayan texts say that the sky is supported by trees and by the upraised arms of the gods, positioned at the four points of the compass. These quadrants are colored black, white, yellow, and red.

❧ Aztec thinkers and philosophers believed that the one reality was an all-embracing supernatural being, half male, half female and who dwelled in the topmost of the layered heavens. This being, or force, is perceived to be the unity of opposites. They called it the Lord and Lady of Duality. All else, they said, is illusion. Coincidentally, the Sanskrit word for illusion is *maya*. The Chinese also conceived of the unity of opposites, expressed by the entwined symbols yin and yang, male and female, half white, half black.

❧ The highly educated artists-scribes were charged with the exacting responsibility of interpreting important information into visual form. There were both female and male artists, who had discernible styles, and proudly signed their work. These are cultures that truly revered their artists.

❧ The first explorers to reach the North Pole drank almost nothing but cocoa on the way. The Aztec warriors drank *cacao*, which sustained them on their marches. And Cortez said it helped his soldiers fight fatigue.

❧ A police dispatcher told me that when dealing with the stress of emergency calls, she and her fellow workers nibble chocolate for its calming and comforting effect. "It really works," she reports. I know what she means.

❧ *Theobroma* "food of the gods," was named by Swedish naturalist Linnaeus (1707–1778)

❧ Coffee, though not officially a sacred tree, would run a close tie to chocolate in the worshipful affections of the multitudes. Coffee has rituals (among others, the coffee break), pet names (jo and java), and houses of worship (coffee houses); for as overheard in a coffee house, "If coffee were a religion, this place would be its temple."

Be creative. The world would be a better place if everybody had a sacred tree, whichever one it might be. Pass it on.

How to Make Chocolate (in case you run out)

1. Cut pods, remove beans, slip off their sweet, white, edible pulp.

2. Ferment beans in warm dark place for 5 or 6 days. Turn them occasionally. (Fermenting reduces bitterness.) Beans must germinate to get that special chocolate flavor.

3. Spread beans out on mats in the sun for one week.

4. Roast beans for 70 to 115 minutes at 215 degrees (for flavor and aroma). For cocoa powder, increase temperature to 250 degrees.

5. Winnow away the thin skins so only the beans remain.

6. Crush, then grind beans into thick paste. Store. (Add other ingredients later.)

7. If you want it sweet, add cocoa butter (fat from beans) and some sugar.

Pass this formula on in your will to assure its continuance for future chocolate lovers.

Connections

Tree Songs

Interspecies Conversations

*"...and to my listening ears, all nature sings and
'round me rings the music of the spheres."*

There is powerful solace in the friendship of trees. The silent ones, sheltering, patient, protective, kin from another kingdom: the kingdom of plants. They can heal and they can communicate. Haven't we experienced among our human friends times of deep communion without words? That's the way it happens with trees, wordlessly, on a very subtle level. But it does happen. Shamans do it— and so can we.

Interspecies communication, especially with animals has been studied for years. Books have been written about communicating with chimpanzees, dolphins, dogs, and parrots, and we can easily relate to this possibility, because we are also animals. We share similar physical traits, such as warm bodies, faces, voices, emotions, thoughts, feelings, and levels of measurable intelligence. Those of us who have animal pets know very well that we communicate with them. With plants it's a little different, they don't have faces (though pansies always seem to be looking back at you,) and carry on their life functions very quietly, it would seem. I'll tell you more about that in a minute.

But first, consider all those stories of dolphins saving shipwrecked sailors by nudging them afloat. In ancient Greece the singer Arion,

Instantly a flood of energy rushed and flowed through my whole body from the tree. It was overwhelming, yet felt friendly with a quality I can only describe as kindness.

captured by pirates, was granted one last song. Dolphins came alongside as he sang. Arion jumped into the sea and was carried by them safely to shore. Dolphins still do such things today. Dr. John Lilly studied their squeak-whistle language to communicate with them, but found them so intelligent that in pity, he finally released these friends from their experimental tank.

(One of the most thrilling experiences of my life happened while I was paddling a kayak in the ocean off the big island of Hawaii. A fleet of gleaming spinner dolphins came racing and leaping towards me. I yipped and jumped into the water to be with them, never fearing for a second that they might harm me with their powerful bodies or that I might drown in the deep water. I just trusted them, delighting in the joy of being so close.)

Now, however, on to contacting trees. Shamans across the planet *do* communicate with trees and other plants to gain specific healing from them. Yet the rest of us needn't become shamans to enjoy the thrill of connecting with a tree. It doesn't take years of study, and it's not a self-conscious thing. To illustrate, I will tell you a true story.

It was a pleasant day in early summer. I stepped outside with a bucket and sponge to wash the kitchen windows near an old oak tree. Strains of beautiful music wafted from the kitchen radio. I stopped a moment to listen, my hand resting lightly on the tree's hard gray trunk. Instantly a flood of energy rushed and flowed through my whole body from the tree. It was overwhelming, yet felt friendly with a quality I can only describe as kindness. I patted the tree, saying, "So you like that music too." It all seemed so natural. But, believe me, there was no mistaking it, the tree loved that music too. I knew it. And it was deliberately "telling" me so. It was connecting with me.

The music ended. I dashed inside, grabbed a scrap of paper to scribble its title and name of the composer. Then slowly I sat down, staring at the words, reading and re-reading what I had just written, trying to comprehend what had just happened.

The name of the music was, "The Ancient Tree" from a suite called, *Spirit Murmurs.*

In that rare moment in time our spirits, the oak's and mine, had crossed an invisible boundary and touched. Our meeting was like two rivers flowing together, merging into a third greater river that carried the composer's deeply felt intention.

Later, when I researched the composer, Alan Hovhaness, it turned out that he did write with deliberate spiritual intent. How marvelous that we hear it in his music.

Those of us who have had a favorite tree to climb, to swing from, to lie beneath, or to tell our troubles to will always remember them with the fondness of old friends.

Test this idea by raising the subject of favorite trees when dinner party conversation lags, and watch how the mood changes. You might try telling the story I will tell you next.

Bea Agins, an anthropologist I met, told me of a strange vision she had of a pink dolphin. She even painted a picture of it. That vision, she said, changed the course of her life.

"But I thought dolphins were gray not pink," she said. "What could this mean?"

Then she discovered that in the Amazon River basin of South America there is a preserve where the pink dolphins swim. "It was a sign," she said. "I was being called to make a journey to the Amazon jungle." Before long she was off to South America.

Bea described the setting: As she waited on the boat dock, jungle sounds droned from the dense undergrowth edging the fast-flowing river, and a bright blue parrot cawed from a nearby tree. It was there she met Ramon who was returning to his tribe up river. He was a shaman, a *curandero.*

Though they could only speak through an interpreter, they quickly became friends. At the same time, they seemed to understand each other without words. She told him about the pink dolphin vision and also of a dream she had in which a plant sings. Ramon beamed, nodding enthusiastically. The songs are called *icaros* he told her.

"Does each plant have a song?" she asked. He answered with eyes and heart, "Yes!" And from that moment on he would become her teacher, and she would learn the plant healing secrets of his tribe.

Ramon's tribe had been dwindling. The youth were no longer interested in the old tribal ways. So the ancient wisdom was in danger of disappearing.

Who would inherit and save this valuable knowledge? Would she agree to be the one? She felt the heavy weight of responsibility and asked to be given time to consider. After deep soul searching over a period of time, at last she agreed. "I felt guided to do this work," she says. "He is entrusting me with this wisdom because I am receptive. Yet the intent was not for me to become a shaman, but rather to record and preserve the ancient wisdom for the good of humanity."

Ramon showed her how to sing to trees and plants to coax their help. He allowed her to record him singing to certain plants. These recordings

"Does each plant have a song?" she asked. He answered with eyes and heart, "Yes!" and from that moment on he would become her teacher and she would learn the plant healing secrets of his tribe.

Tree Songs

she brought back to California where she kindly allowed me to listen to Ramon sing to the plants. The old shaman's voice is soft, peaceful, like a lullaby, and has an innocent singsong, flute-like quality. He sort of whistles off the sound at the end of a phrase.

Here's what I learned from Bea: "The *curanderos* of the Amazon are keepers of these sacred plant treasures, their healing remedies, and the spirit of their songs (*icaros*), and [they] receive information from the plant's spirit. Each plant has unique energies or vibrations. It is important to be in relationship with the 'beingness' of [a plant's] life force. Then the shaman translates these frequencies into songs that can be taught to an apprentice." When the music is repeated over and over, a sort of "charm" happens that releases the plant's medicine. The shaman then receives information from the plant's spirit.

Permission to extract healing must first be requested of the plant's "owner" (the plant's spirit).

Bea told me that since plants don't speak words, each of us will receive impressions from plants in our own ways. This is because we are all just a little different and are good at some things and not good at others.

Being a shaman is not an easy line of work. If no apprentices can be found to carry on, this wisdom will soon be lost.

Being a shaman is not an easy line of work. If no apprentices can be found to carry on, this wisdom will soon be lost. Yet, there are other scholars intensely interested in preserving it. The findings of these scholars reinforce the importance of music.

Anthropologist Dr. Michael Harner says that for a plant's medicine to work, the person's connecting with the plant's spirit is more important than even eating the plant. He says learning a plant's song opens communication. Songs invoke the power of the plant to come forth. If the person is not healed and the medicine doesn't work, it is because the plant's spirit hasn't been invoked. But here's a curious thing: The physical form of the plant doesn't have to be present for a person to be healed by that plant's medicine. Only its spirit is needed. And its songs are the invitation.

In the words of another dedicated anthropologist, Eliot Cowan, who modestly calls himself an "apprentice shaman," "It's not the plant, but the spirit of the plant that heals."

The spirits are out there waiting to help us, if we will just ask. The spirit stays in the plant after it's picked, sometimes for as long as eight months.

"Even though we endanger them," says Cowan, "the continued generosity of plants towards our species and to their fellow creatures is absolutely remarkable.

"We are made of dirt, rain, sunshine, minerals, and gasses. . . . Ecological crisis is bad for us all. The plants already know this . . . the fortune of one is the fortune of all . . . that is why they are generous and compassionate with humankind." (Cowan 1995)

So, we need plants but they don't need us. Considering our indifference to and often brutal treatment of them, their willingness to give us a tendril up is pure benevolence.

But unlike humankind, plants know they are part of creation and live in harmony.

Dr. David Abram, a cultural anthropologist/philosopher, says, "The most learned and powerful shaman will be the one who has first learned his or her skills directly from the land itself, from a specific animal or plant, from a river or storm, during a prolonged sojourn out beyond the boundaries of the human society. . . . In indigenous, oral cultures, nature itself speaks. . . . The human voice . . . voices of wolves, wind and waves are in discourse with the 'animate earth.'"

After Words

- Ah-ho-san-go, spirit of Ajosacha (main plant of the Ashual Indians of the Amazon), dresses in a crown of feathers . . . a beautiful necklace made of the rainbow . . . looks like an old wizened white man. He is the protector . . . providing good dreams. He is always called in to protect the shaman before a session, during the healing and at the close, ensuring protection for all concerned. His presence feels gentle and comforting.

- A student of Cowan's says, "The spirit appeared to me as a jolly muscular little man, full of fun and kindness." (That word "kindness" pops up repeatedly in sources across the world.)

- Another of Cowan's students, Dr. Gil Milner, says, "Oh, it's the song of the plant. . . . Each plant gives you its power in the form of a song . . . and they have words." He picked up a drum and played a slow, loping rhythm and then began to sing.

- Watering my garden one morning, humming a quiet song, it occurred to me to offer my song to the garden. A silence fell, a marking of time . . . I knew all the plants were listening.

- It turns out that the composer Alan Hovhaness, as a spiritual seeker, had a psychic reading from Edgar Cayce, a connection I, too, have.

- Jane Goodall, Dr. John C. Lilly, and Rupert Sheldrake are pioneers in animal communication. Clive Backster is a pioneer in plant communication. Peter Tompkins and Christopher Bird were both remarkable investigators. And there are many others.

The Forest People

Excerpts from anthropologist Colin M. Turnbull's
exquisite work *The Forest People* (1961)

Hidden within the damp, dark dripping tropical rain forest of Africa's Congo River Basin lies the Ituri Forest. It is home to the Mbuti Pygmies, one of Africa's oldest tribes, who have lived there for thousands of years. But let Turnbull describe it in his own words:

"It is full of delicate colors and shades and whispering sounds, and up in the highest branches orchids shyly hide their heads among the moss. It is a cool restful, shady world with light filtering lazily through the tree tops that meet high overhead, shutting out direct sunlight."

In contrast, not far away, village dwellers live in plantation clearings cut from the forest. Their surroundings are hot, dusty and dirty. They fight a constant battle against the forest's intrusion because the planted fields they labor so painfully to cultivate soon become depleted. Then they must abandon these fields to dig new ones, "for the soil that supports the primeval forest with luxurious ease, refuses to bear fruit to the crops of the villagers for more than three consecutive years," says Turnbull.

The village dwellers rarely enter the forest, afraid of the "dark dripping silence." They fear malevolent spirits there and are deeply suspicious.

But, says Turnbull, "The forest is better and kinder than the outside world that threatens to destroy it. This world is good and without evil." He says the Pygmies "know the secret language that is denied all outsiders."

The Pygmies say, "No need to fear anything. When we are the Children of the Forest what need have we to be afraid of it?" In sensing and understanding subtle forest changes, Turnbull says, "just at a time that leopards would be prowling about in search of food, the Pygmies were unwilling to disturb the forest or the animals it concealed. It was as if they were a part of the silence and darkness of the forest itself."

The Pygmies' songs echo this refrain, and, Turnbull says of their mysterious Molimo ritual, "I could hardly distinguish their music from the music of the crickets and frogs and the birds of the night. Something wonderful had come into their lives and filled them with magic, love, and trust."

A Pygmy explains, "When something goes wrong it must be because the Forest is sleeping and not looking after its children; so what do we do? We wake it up by singing to it so it awakens happy. When our world is going well, we sing to it. Then also we sing to the forest because we want it to share our happiness."

At no time do Pygmies ask for this or that. All that's needed is to awaken the forest and everything will come right. The villagers, on the other hand, have a different point of view. When things go wrong, it must surely be that an evil spirit, a witch, or a sorcerer has cursed them. So then a ritual must be performed to appease the curser.

"The Pygmies' logic is simpler and their faith stronger, because their world is kinder," says Turnbull. "Of their God, they say, 'He must be good to give us so many things. He must be of the forest.'"

Though conflicts or petty grievances occasionally disrupt community harmony, their mutual needs demand getting along. But as a last resort, there are two things a Pygmy cannot endure: mocking laughter or exile." Eventually, in contrition, the exiled will return to the group, where some form of appropriate forgiveness happens.

Amazingly, "they have no chiefs, no lawgivers, no leaders. The forest, the great provider, is the one standard by which all deeds and thoughts are judged. It is the lawgiver, the leader, the final arbiter."

Turnbull, wanting to explore some other areas a long drive away, took along Kenge, his Pygmy friend and guide, saying to him that it was

When something goes wrong it must be because the Forest is sleeping and not looking after its children.

no more than a day's drive from the last of the trees. Kenge, replied, "No trees! No trees at all?" Kenge was going to have nothing to do with savages who lived in a land without trees.

After returning from their trip, Turnbull says, "back in the forest I was profoundly content. As we entered once more into the shade of the great friendly old trees, Kenge said, 'This is the real world. This is a good world.' Then commenting on a kindly Catholic priest they had met in the outside world, Kenge said, 'his God must be the same as our God of the forest; it must be one God.'"

Another time, Turnbull told this story of a dying tree: "I noticed a huge old tree with great buttress roots joining the trunk some 15 feet above the ground. It was completely dead standing up white and naked among all the greenery, its lifelessness all the more pitiable in the midst of such luxuriance. Giving it a critical look, Kenge said, 'it should just miss our house.'

"One night we were awakened by a sharp cracking sound, followed by a loud groan. I lay for hours listening to cracks as sharp as a rifle going off, and intermittent groaning. It got louder and more continuous. Then just as I cleared the doorway, the old tree came down. Slowly, reluctantly, clutching at all the lesser trees that stood in its way. They were living and it was dead. It smashed its way on downward to the ground. The tremendous din of its collapse was followed by a light pattering of broken branches and twigs, then silence. 'You see,' said Kenge, 'it did miss our house.' Then Turnbull points out, "but only by about 6 feet."

The exquisite contrast between the Forest People and our nature-deprived civilized selves is wonderfully shown in the following story:

"I think I learned just how far away we civilized human beings have drifted from reality," says Turnbull. "The moon was full . . . I heard a curious noise . . . and wandered over to see what it was. There in the tiny clearing, splashed with silver was the sophisticated Kenge, clad in bark cloth, adorned with leaves, a flower stuck in his hair. He was all alone, dancing around and singing softly to himself as he gazed up into the treetops. I asked jokingly why he was dancing alone. He stopped, slowly turned around and looked at me as though I was the biggest fool he had ever seen . . . plainly surprised by my stupidity. 'But I am not dancing alone!' he said. 'I am dancing with the forest, dancing with the moon.' Then he ignored me and continued his dance of love and life."

Pygmies "know the secret that is denied all outsiders."

The Forest People

After Words

🐦 In the years since the 1961 publication of Turnbull's widely acclaimed book, *The Forest People*, the Pygmies and Bantu villagers eventually intermarried for reasons of mutual survival. But wars in neighboring countries and migration have devastated the forest and threatened to destroy the Pygmies entirely. Turnbull's study captured something rare and beautiful, as in a time capsule, giving us a glimpse of humans living harmoniously in nature.

🐦 The precious trees of the Ituri Forest are being cut down for their beautiful wood or to make way for the ever 'hungry' crop or grazing lands, just as tropical forests across the planet are being leveled, hastening the inevitable global climate changes that are already altering our own lives.

🐦 In neighboring Kenya, Wangari Maathai, PhD. in Veterinary Medicine, received the 2004 Nobel Peace Prize for "her contribution to sustainable development, democracy, and peace." Elected Member of Parliament, she served as Assistant Minister for Environment, Natural Resources, and Wildlife. She founded the Green Belt Movement, a communty-based organization of women who have planted at least 40 million trees in Kenya to stop erosion, reduce poverty, and encourage conservation!

🐦 "How do we know to gather together, without telephones or other kinds of communication? We touch the trees and the trees send the message." (Elder, Raven Indian Tribe, Alaska)

When I am studying plants,
I feel like I am talking with some kind of supernatural life,
like I am talking with someone who does not speak.

Cornielle Ewango, Forest Conservationist,
Ituri Forest of Eastern Congo

The most common trait of all indigenous peoples
is a reverence for the life-giving earth, and the Native
American shared this elemental ethic: The land was
alive to his loving touch, and he, its son, was brother
to all creatures. His feelings were made visible in
medicine bundles and dance rhythms for rain, and all
of his religious rites and land attitudes savored the
inseparable world of nature and God, the master of
Life. During the long Indian tenure the land remained
undefiled save for scars no deeper than the scratches
of cornfield clearings or the farming canals of the
Hohokams on the Arizona desert.

Stewart Lee Udall

Nature Spirits

Hold on to your socks. There are people among us, rational people, who see and hear nature spirits. If we should happen to pass any one of them, we would see nothing unusual about them. If we happen to chat with one of them, they wouldn't let on: They have learned to keep their abilities to themselves. We would too, since we know how public opinion regards such things. Most paranormal experiences are private and precious.

But the nature spirits need our cooperation these days. That these subtle beings co-exist is worth knowing. And we'll be in excellent company.

For instance, the Irish scholar, Ella Young, knew nature spirits. Dorothy MacLean and Peter Caddy of Findhorn, Scotland did too, as did Edgar Cayce in the United States, and the scientist-philosopher Rudolf Steiner in Austria. Even I have "heard" them sometimes. My friend Jan Peck saw them as "little spinning vortices" as we walked in the woods.

Dr. Rudolf Steiner said, "There exists a spiritual world, comprehensible to pure thinking, but which is fully accessible only to the higher faculties of knowledge latent in us all. . . . There is a real spiritual world, and elemental beings which surround us . . . the Hierarchies, the Angels,

Archangels and so on. The world is inhabited with concrete spiritual content, with spiritual powers and spiritual beings. It is not a matter of indifference to these things living in the spiritual world that we know about them. . . . It is as if they were deprived of some spiritual nourishment when men here on earth know nothing about them. The spiritual world is in close connection with this earthly physical world."

Machaelle Wright of Perelandra, a nature research center in Virginia, "sees" and "hears" the invisible forces of nature and works with them. She says that she has experienced nature spirits as "swirling spheres of light energy," and has walked through the woods with one of these balls of energy beside her. It moved straight through a tree and out the other side while she moved around it. She says that her personal inner vision, "lies in the area of energy," which she sees in waves. When a " nature intelligence" chose to be visible to her, out of regard it used a context with which she was comfortable: *energy.*

We will each deal with the unseen world in a way that our minds can accept.

When nature spirits wish to appear to us, they use our stored memories, pictures that have influenced us. We all make thought pictures (thought forms) that release into the atmosphere around us. Nature spirits use these images for creating a temporary "body" in which to appear. That is, if they choose to reveal themselves. Seeing them is a gift; so consider yourself fortunate if you have had the privilege. I'm still waiting, but since I've seen ghosts of people and pets, there may still be hope.

A word of caution. Our imaginations can give nature spirits emotional characteristics like our own. "So if we think elves can be mean," says Machaelle, "we'll create a mean elf." Yet love and balance flow from nature spirits, and Machaelle says she has always felt care and protection coming from them, never fear or apprehension on her part.

I too have felt only benevolence emanating from nature, never anger or pettiness, though once I was "advised" by my rosebush not to pay more attention to its bug-damaged leaves than to the beauty of its flowers. The clear message was: Don't dwell on the negative; simply note the damage, correct it, and move on. Lessons of wisdom from a rosebush.

Did I actually "hear" words? Yes, in a way. The thoughts got sorted out in my mind in the form of words. But not words in sequence as you would speak to someone, rather simultaneously, as thoughts come to us, all at once.

There exists a spiritual world, comprehensible to pure thinking, but which is fully accessible only to the higher faculties of knowledge latent in us all.

Do these messages come often? No, only when I'm free of other thoughts. They have to compete with mind-chatter.

Do nature spirits help even if you can't contact them? Yes, it's their job you might say. But our willing attitude and good intentions help a lot to create harmonious conditions. Those who know say nature spirits are eager to assist.

Why should we consider contacting nature spirits? Because it is deeply satisfying to connect with other kingdoms of nature and other dimensions too. It makes life richer, and when you are enriched, everyone benefits just a little more. Besides, it is really fun.

With a little help from nature spirits, planting a garden becomes a co-creative process: We plant and water, they grow, everybody benefits.

Say you want to grow birch trees. Well, since each plant has its own spirit, its own quality, its own needs, and its own *deva* (day'-vah), go out and ask the spirit of the birch tree to advise you on where it would like to grow, in what soil, and how much sun and watering it will need. In return, it will give you insights, information that will come as thought impressions. The process is easier when we get quiet to receive the message. Meditation helps. The trick is not to work at it too hard. Relax and let it flow.

Machaelle advises that when dealing with *devas,* state precisely what you need. Always contact the *deva* of that particular plant and don't worry about whether or not the contact is working. See what happens.

"Their love is the love of action and purpose," she says, "and that's what they want from us . . . appropriate action done in a caring spirit.

"The *deva* supplies the consciousness or soul input that gives to a tree its definition, direction, and purpose," (like an architect drawing up plans).

"The *nature spirit* level builds the structure according to the plans and maintains that structure throughout its whole life cycle," (like a carpenter or builder-caretaker).

But there is trouble on Earth. Machaelle says, "It has gotten so bad over the past fifty years that nature spirits have for the most part, responded by withdrawing from vast areas of land . . . thrown off balance by the ecological imbalance surrounding it. Most of the farmlands around the world are now without nature spirits. Without them the quality and amount of energy is at its minimum, allowing just enough energy for the form to remain. Empty form, food without light." Could this be why so much of our food is tasteless?

Their love is the love of action and purpose and that's what they want from us . . .

Nature Spirits

We need the nature spirits, but they don't need us. If humankind disappeared from the face of the earth, there would likely be a great sigh of relief from nature.

I remember the question asked by the Balinese musicians: "Where are your tree spirits?" The answer might be that they've retreated because of our disregard.

Machaelle says, "When nature spirits leave an area they congregate somewhere not frequented by man, often a woods. They'll make it impassable with dead trees and overgrown vines."

The teachers at Findhorn in Scotland suggested that if we have a bit of unused land, we could help out the nature spirits by setting aside a little preserve for them, a safe haven, untrammeled and undisturbed, the view of which will remind us to tread lightly.

As the Irish say when thanked for a kindness, "Ah, but it takes so little."

After Words

- When Edgar Cayce was a child he played with fairies and elves. Later in life he said, "Brownies are as definite entities as man, materialized . . . and are only seen by those who are attuned to the infinite."

- Poison oak: It was a fine day out on the Marin headlands overlooking the Golden Gate Bridge and the vast Pacific Ocean. I sat cross-legged, sketching plant life, then stopped to admire a poison oak shrub a short itching-distance away. It was a handsome, thriving plant dressed in autumn red. Feeling magnanimous I closed my eyes to contact its spirit and send it love. Immediately came the message, Ha! You can't love me but you can respect me.

- Useful thought: No green thumb? Try planting a little plot of crabgrass. It will grow, that is a certainty. You will succeed because crabgrass succeeds; try wrestling it out of your lawn. Tenacity and relentless persistence are qualities one could assign to the virtually indestructible crabgrass. Truly inspiring. One might even adopt crabgrass as a personal symbol to emblazon on a banner to instill confidence. I can see it now . . .

- Thomas Moore wrote, "You have a soul; the tree in front of your house has a soul. . . . I paid a visit to the old homestead where two grand chestnut trees offered shade and beauty for over fifty years . . . [they] had not lost their nobility and kindliness. If someone thinking of widening the road or building a new house should ever come to cut down those chestnut trees, it would be a painful loss . . . not just because the trees are symbols of time past, but because they are living beings and surrounded by a huge aura of memory. . . . They are part of the family, bound to us as individuals of another species. . . . We can only treat badly those things whose souls we disregard. . . . This world is our home. . . . Our responsibility to it comes not from obligation or logic but from true affection."

The mighty crabgrass

The Fairy Music

The gods of Mammon and Mars (crass materialism and war) have never been the patrons of a great age. What is lacking? Beauty, truth, solitude and the comradeship of the nature gods. We have bartered away body, soul, and spirit for a push-button existence, and the right to crow from every dung-hill. (Ella Young)

Though Ella Young was a highly respected scholar in her field at the university, few people knew the other side of her life outside of academic circles. For Ella was gifted with the ability to see into other realms. Her combined intellectual and psychic abilities make these revelations especially fascinating.

After a radio interview in which she was reading from her works, the interviewer began casually asking her questions about the other realms that he had been told she knew and understood. The tape was still running.

He asked her about the possibility of communicating with trees.

She seemed to trust that her questioner was sincere and answered him directly in her cultured, Irish voice, "Well, when you open a line of communication with a tree it sends out words. It did to me as I was passing by. But they generally don't. Redwoods in particular send out a very lovely feeling. Then, if you have friends among the earth spirits, sunlight would come [where there was none before]. And perhaps some golden leaves would fall, things like that. But you see, you can't expect anything at all. If you really love the thing, be content. Otherwise you fall into the trap of asking for phenomena. . . . [This means the demanding of proof, which breaks the spell of connection.] You just love that tree, want to love it more and come closer to it. You don't go for something it can say to you. What you get from it is beyond the intellect. It's the transcendent consciousness that connects you. [When you make a connection], then quite suddenly everything changes. You can see colors, but more, a sense of oneness with that thing. You get the sense that you both are divinity."

The interviewer urged her on, asking, "Are there trees that you cannot love, and that are not friendly?"

She answered, "Well, if you can't love them then leave them alone. Always begin with the things you love, since not everything and not everybody is loveable . . . But the Great Brotherhood, the one you really could have, is the brotherhood of the animals, the angels, the earth, the stones, the trees, and all good humans of course. These are the things you can love.

"As for trees, I once got in touch with a giant sequoia tree in Yosemite. But you'd have to be alone, or with someone who had the same purpose. Be content with whatever you get. If you really want to connect with it, you might sleep there, as close as you can to it. You just relax. Don't tense up, because that's not the part of yourself that gets it."

The interviewer asked if one could request words from nature spirits.

Young said, "You don't go to a thing for something it can say to you. What it gives you is something beyond intelligence.

"You see, neither time nor space exists for thought. Thought goes instantly. You can greet the thing without even being there and it will know."

The interviewer asked if evil spirits lurk in nature.

"No," she answered thoughtfully, "I have never come in contact with evil spirits. Any evil would come in the form of a person that might come and foul or poison a place perhaps. Now you could come in contact with beings so powerful that they might destroy you just as lightning would. But lightning isn't evil. [In fact], if you were a being of a higher type, lightning would only exhilarate you."

Then the interviewer asked her about the fairy music.

"In Ireland, many hear the fairy music. I heard it in Sausalito, California, too. They [the little people] have far more instruments than any orchestra, but it varies so. Violins, voices sweeter than humans, there are great clanging bells and shouting in maddest joy. There are pipes, anvils and small tinkling bells. But sometimes it's the litany of a Gregorian chant. I believe it is everywhere. I heard the words, *ak batha*, but didn't know what it meant." She said it is possible to hear it if you are a person who is receptive.

Then he asked: "If California had been lived in as long as Ireland has, would there be sacred places here, too?"

"But it's not the being lived in; it's the fact of the nature spirits being there. For instance, there are magic places where fountain waters come up out of the earth. The old Druids were capable of recognizing those places, and very often, put their temples there because of what came out of the earth. You see, when you are in a magic place, you are more conditioned to be receptive to it. And so, the place becomes sacred to the people who recognize it. It's good to make a pilgrimage to a sacred place. The sacred places like your coming there. It stirs something in you, and the nature spirits like your comradeship. The [American] Indians are often protected because they have made the Great Comradeship with the land."

The interviewer wanted to know, "Does the United States have sacred places?"

"This is the most magical country I've ever been in, outside of Ireland. The land is living. There are tremendous, powerful, magnificent beings here. Archangels, you'd call them if you saw them. It's the fact of the nature spirits being there" [that makes it sacred]. The interviewer coaxed her on.

"You see, when you are in a magic place you are more likely to be receptive to it," she continued, "and so the place becomes sacred to the people who recognize it." Her dignified voice was so matter-of-fact, the subject almost seemed common talk.

The interviewer asked, "How do you know a sacred place if you're not psychic?"

"In a sacred place, there is a way for people who aren't so psychic to know that there was something special there. They might say, "Oh, the sun has come out!" And they would feel so happy. It's the divinity of the place. But when a divinity leaves a sacred place, there can be heard an enormous sound in the night, though nothing may have changed to the normal eye. Yet a sensitive would know it had gone, because the feeling of the place had become ordinary."

But lightning isn't evil. [In fact], if you were a being of a higher type, lightning would only exhilarate you."

This radio interview with Ella Young was the most asked for in the history of radio station KPFA, Berkeley, California. Ella Young was a scholar, writer, poet, lecturer, and revolutionary. She was holder of the Chair of Celtic Mythology and Folklore at the University of California, Berkeley.

After Words

- Ella Young died in 1956. With her spirit fresh in our minds, it's useful to remember that the doors to other realms can be accessed through meditation, or a spontaneous knowing, or through a trance state, or in the dream state.

- I had a vivid prophetic dream many years ago, in three parts. Two parts have already come true, and they changed my life. In the first, a man I knew as a friend, catches up with me, hiking up a hill, takes my hand, and says, "Let's go on the journey together." He became my husband of thirty-plus years. The second: I labor up to a mountain's top and find I've won a prize that will also benefit others. (I later won the California Supreme Court case: Preston v. State Board of Equalization, benefiting all California artists, as well as publishers.) Here is the third part:
  I am hiking over a sunlit hill. From a little bush to my side comes the shaking of tiny bells. With a certainty I know this to be the laughter of elves. I can hear them still. Was this the third true thing, a glimpse into another reality? I believe it was.

- Meditating with a group in the king's chamber of the Giza pyramid, I heard a heavenly chorus chanting Gregorian-like music. When my critical mind questioned, it stopped, but it began again as soon as I put my reasoning mind aside. Some others heard different kinds of chanting, while one heard a long, sonorous sound, another heard Tibetan monks chanting. The experience was thrilling to each of us, yet felt perfectly natural. Others in our group heard nothing, for reasons I didn't explore.

- During a monthly meditation meeting, while I was entering meditation, I heard the sharp meowing of our hostess's cat Pie. Later I asked where he was. He had died the previous week.

- The famous teacher Ram Dass (Richard Alpert), while meditating alone heard many voices chanting "OM." His guru later told him he had tuned into the *om-kar,* a sort of sound stream coming from all the sincere meditators down the centuries that had ever chanted this sound. Countless others have experienced this phenomenon. Have you?

The Findhorn Experiment

O n a sandy wind-whipped spit of land, salted by the cold North Sea, far in the north of Scotland three adults and three little boys began a magical adventure. It was November 1962. The people: Peter and Eileen Caddy, their three children, and their colleague Dorothy McLean. The place: Findhorn, a caravan park. The reason: They had been "led" there, but they didn't know their assignment.

For the previous ten years every action of their lives had been directed by the "voice of God." They trusted that if they were faithful to it, all their needs would be met and the nature of their work at Findhorn revealed. This was their test. A guiding belief they held was to love where you are, who you are with, and what you are doing. And to always give thanks.

While awaiting guidance from the "voice within," they put their energies to work. Though the harsh conditions and infertile soil mocked their efforts, they planted a small garden. They dug trenches a foot deep and 18 inches wide, adding chopped beach grass, seaweed, and manure to make it fertile. A compost heap was created of rotting vegetation and wood ash that, as it decomposed, would turn into new soil that then could be added to the garden. And they planted seeds.

They were "told" to direct light and love into the soil with their spades as they turned the clods of dirt. "It was like connecting up negative and positive poles in electricity," said Peter. "The energy flowed through me to the earth." Then Dorothy made contact with the *devas,* the plant spirits, life force personified, part of the angelic hierarchy that holds the pattern for each species and directs the energy to form a plant. The results were spectacular.

Soon the the little group was excitedly getting practical daily advice on every aspect of gardening from the plants themselves. But what's more, they began harvesting gigantic vegetables, a 42-pound cabbage and one broccoli plant too heavy to lift, that fed them for months and that were bursting with flavor and vitality. Now they could sell the overflow of their abundant organically grown crops to eager buyers who were delighted with the taste and quality.

News spread. Visitors came. Everyone was excited (including the plant *devas* who, they said, wanted to be part of the cooperative venture between the human and nature kingdoms). The other people did not yet know about the *deva* factor. But this news was too important to keep to themselves any longer. So, at last, cautiously, they told of the wonderful teachings they received from the *devas* and that it was possible for everyone to do as they had. And that it would benefit both kingdoms and the world at large.

People came from across the world to live at Findhorn to learn the process. My friend Jan Peck from Mill Valley, California, went, reporting back to us of her experiences there. Some Findhorn stories are absolutely priceless. For instance: It occasionally happened that someone would offend a plant spirit by cutting away blossoms the plant required to house its elf population. Then a little ceremony would be held and an apology offered. After all, people were new at this stuff.

R. O. Crombie, a sensitive who could see the invisible world, said of the episode that he found himself "surrounded by a throng of little gorse elves all aflurry."

Today, the emphasis at Findhorn has shifted toward "the flowering of human consciousness." Meditation and study groups are regularly conducted there, and interestingly, their study is along a more ecological and scientific path. For instance, there is a project for the reforestation of Scotland. My Scottish-born father, a naval architect, would have approved, since those forests had been harvested to build the ships his own father, a ship's master-carpenter, worked, and his forefathers sailed, and ships my father continued to design. A kind of making right.)

Yes, reports say the gardens are still tended by successive waves of temporary and live-in folks. But the giant vegetables, having served their purpose of calling attention, are now what a good gardener would call: Providing for their caretakers.

Lest we regret those early days of magic decades ago, as with all things, change is inevitable. Dynamics shift. Situations, institutions, and human interactions are always repositioning. But the great cogs that work an ordered universe remain in place. The *devas* of the plant kingdom still perform their functions as ever. And wherever a single soul reaches across the unseen to make a connection, it happens.

The devas of the plant kingdom still perform their functions as ever.

The Findhor Experiment

The Giving Tree

Leaning on the deck rail of my little Sausalito house one spring day, straining to see through the upper leaves of a large tree obscuring the hill beyond, I wished idly that if only the top two feet of the tree were gone my view could be restored. Within the next few days, leaves began dropping from the top of the tree, but only from the top two feet. A few days later the last leaf dropped from that area of the tree. I could once again see the hill across the valley.

It became apparent, a couple of weeks later that no more leaves were going to follow, that the remaining lower leaves were intact, healthy, and secured. Then it dawned on me that something utterly remarkable had happened. I caught my breath in confusion and amazement. Was this possible? There, indeed, was the view I had wished for. It was as if the tree had "understood" and granted my wish. A thrilling idea.

I was grateful. But as time passed, I became uneasy, for even though I couldn't have expected what happened, the tree had granted my wish at its own expense. I read once that a tree's topmost leaves are unique in that they protect it in some way, processing the sun's energy differently from its other leaves.

After telling a few friends this story and showing them the empty top branches, some were silent and some squinty-eyed. Cold observation proved the tree to be bare on top. "Right, it's bare on top," they would say and point out possible reasons, "Not enough water?"

Pretty soon the novelty turned into concern for the tree's well-being. I wanted those leaves back more than I wanted the view. I went out and pleaded with the tree to grow the leaves back, and said that I was really sorry to have caused it any harm.

Slowly, to my great relief, buds started reappearing on the empty branches, tiny ones at first, only a scattering of green here and there. Then more and more popped open and stretched into leaves. Within a short time the treetop was filled with beautiful new green leaves. I was weak with gratitude. Friends now marveled to see the perfectly normal tree. The rationalizers still rationalized. But I knew what I knew.

I had a friend back then named Francis Rath who, prior to becoming a bookstore owner, had been a rather imposing law enforcement officer. He found that in the course of his work, when he put his hands on people in trauma, they would instantly stop convulsing and breathe normally; he was a true healer and a sensitive. Francis came to a party at my house more than a year after the leaf-dropping incident. He told me that when he stepped outside for a breather during the evening he had leaned against this tree and felt it to be remarkable. Its emanations were compassionate and giving. Did I know that this was one special tree? I told him the story that I have just told you.

Compassion is no attribute.
It is the Law of Laws . . . a shoreless universal essence,
the light of everlasting right and fitness of all things,
the love of love eternal."

From Buddhism: *The Seven Portals.*

Spirit as Aura

The Link That Connects All Nature

A kindly neighbor took me to the cat lying dead by the side of the road. I said, "That's not my cat," I still marvel that I did not recognize my lovely, golden-eyed tiger cat, but you see, the light had gone from her eyes, empty of her animating spirit. The Tiggy I knew was gone.

"There's a cat dead in the street," I said to Alan, "I think maybe it's Tiggy." He gave me a you-don't-know-your-own-cat? look.

"Please," I said, "Go look, okay?" With noble resignation he got a bag, the kind he had used to collect dead raccoons, possums, and squirrels over the years and did the grim deed. It was Tig, of course. We buried her under an olive tree on the hill below the cabin and told each other stories from her checkered life as we mourned the loss of our beautiful cat friend.

Where did that light go? Is it the same for cats as for humans? Is it the same for mice or trees? It seems to me that this subject holds vastly important clues to the concept of conscious nature. I believe that what is true of our light is true also of trees' light.

I've seen the peach colored glow around an oak tree grove growing on a hill, the trees' outer branches radiant, healthy, and strong outlined against a winter-gray sky. Even the doubting Alan said, "But doesn't everyone see the peach edges around the borders of leaves? There's a peach aura around the new growth, very discernible and real." And it's not just your eye's rods and cones playing tricks.

As far as I know everything living has an aura: people, animals, and plants. So do rocks and amoebas, say skilled seers and shamans. What then actually is an aura? What does it mean that we have them? We all do, you know.

To me, a person's aura looks very much like the glow around a streetlight. It shines outward from the body. Its intensity is bright or dim according to a person's health or strength. It can be in different colors with meanings that can be analyzed.

You've likely seen auras in paintings of Christian saints and holy figures in medieval Western paintings and in portrayals of the Buddha and other holy figures in Oriental art. Sometimes auras are shown surrounding the whole body, maybe gold or multicolored. Other times they are symbolically shown, looking like golden "plates" behind the heads of saints, or as golden rings floating above them. In these cases, the artist is using symbolic "shorthand" for the aura.

Once I saw thousands of exquisitely thin light rays streaming from a woman. It surprised me, as it was so similar to what I had seen in a Fra Angelico painting.

Caroline Myss, PhD, a pioneer in the field of energy medicine, says, "Your physical body is surrounded by an energy field that extends as far out as your outstretched arms and the full length of your body. It is both an information center and a highly sensitive perceptual system. . . . Our spirits, our energy, and our personal power are all one and the same force." She also says, "Your biology is your biography."

Dr. Candace Pert, neurobiologist, says, "Clearly, there's another form of energy that we have not understood. For example, there's a form of energy that leaves the body when the body dies. . . ." Other psychics or sensitives tell of a second "light" body self that continues on after the body we have inhabited dies and is discarded like used shoes or an old car. I think of Tiggy's spent body, her empty eyes.

The psychic Edgar Cayce said, "Ever since I can remember I have seen colors in connection with people . . . blues, greens, and reds gently pouring from their heads and shoulders. . . . I see them change as time

Caroline Myss, PhD, a pioneer in the field of energy medicine, says, "Your physical body is surrounded by an energy field that extends as far out as your outstretched arms and the full length of your body.

goes by; sickness, dejection, love, fulfillment—these are all reflected in the aura, and for me the aura is the weather vane of the soul."

Cayce tells the story of a woman also able to see auras. She was in a department store, about to step into an elevator filled with people when suddenly she was repelled and stepped back. "Something was wrong," she said. "The interior, though lighted, seemed dark to me." Then she realized what had made her uneasy: the people in the elevator had no auras. She turned away, and in the next moment the elevator cable snapped! The car fell crashing to the basement. All the occupants were killed.

It puzzled me that their auras had left before they had. Why? We can conjecture.

But, first, let me tell you a firsthand experience, perhaps not as dramatic, but things that I know. I once saw an angry red aura around a man who wasn't getting his way. This warned me to be wary of him and distance myself.

Haven't we all felt a strong negative reaction to someone at one time or another? These feelings are warnings and well worth paying attention to. Emotions show up in the aura and can be sensed, even if you haven't seen them yet.

You don't need to *see* an aura to perceive its color. You can actually *know* it. This happened to me one summer morning. I was talking casually with a friend out on my deck, when all at once I "knew" without seeing it that her aura was a beautiful sky blue. Ordinarily these observations are best left unsaid to keep from unduly alarming others, but since she was already disposed toward such concepts I told her.

"Oh, yes," she said, " I've often been told this." So she was able to verify that my perception was accurate; my education was expanding.

Another time, at the seashore I watched as a normally obedient dog-friend of mine was unleashed to run loose. Henry the Ecology-Dog (who retrieves discarded beer cans and the Sunday paper,) shot off like a bullet into the rolling surf. As he joyfully leapt and bounded along the shore, his wet black body gleaming, I noticed he was totally enveloped in a bright green aura.

Days later I asked my healer friend Greg Schelkun what that color of green meant. "Hmm," mused Greg. "Is this dog under the strain of much discipline?" I said he was in obedience school. Greg said, "Well, then, he's just expressing his happiness and freedom." Good old dog, I thought, appreciating Henry all the more for his life of dutiful service and admirable self-restraint.

You don't need to see *an aura to perceive its color. You can actually* know *it.*

Spirit as Aura

But to me, there is no question that consciousness continues. In this present physical plane we take on a temporary body "shell" in order to move around in this three-dimensional world. What a pity to mistake the "shell" for the soul. That's like mistaking the car for its driver.

I took a class in seeing auras from Jack Schwarz, the famous "Western yogi," who says anyone can learn to see auras with enough practice and discipline. It did help with technique. Although my best experiences happen spontaneously, focus does improve reception.

Aura as proof of the existence of spirit tells us something very important about our lives, and our deaths.

"Dying doesn't mean we will cease to exist, or even lose consciousness for very long for that matter," says Barbara Ann Brennan, former NASA atmospheric research scientist, who has now become a healer and therapist. "The human energy field isn't just an energy field, it is the person. . . . I can see a person after they have left their physical body at death. . . . They are composed of the higher four levels of their energy bodies without a physical body inside them. The lower three levels that hold the physical body in place dissolve in the dying process. To me death is a transition, . . . a rebirth into another plane of reality."

So everything has an aura, and it is this energy that lives on when our physical bodies have died and turned to dust. Exactly where we go after death is too vast a subject to address here. But to me, there is no question that consciousness continues. In this present physical plane we take on a temporary body "shell" in order to move around in this three-dimensional world. What a pity to mistake the "shell" for the soul. That's like mistaking the car for its driver.

We are inhabiting eternity right now. Our ongoing adventure will therefore continue throughout this marvelous, multidimensional universe. What a blessing. Safe journey!

After Words

- There are 97 different cultures, worldwide that have a name for life energy fields. (White and Krippner 1977)
- Now I understood that what science calls energy is spirit . . . I, too, am energy or spirit. (Schwarz 1992)
- Tree aura colors can vary according to their expression of themselves. (Greg Schelkun, healer)
- Colors reflect the soul and the spirit, the mind and the body, but remember, they indicate lack of perfection, incompleteness. If we were all we should be, pure white would emanate from us, Strive toward that, and when you see it in others, follow it as if it were a star. It is. (Edgar Cayce, *Auras*)

In my investigations on the action of forces on matter,
I was amazed to find boundary lines vanishing and
to discover points of contact emerging between the
Living and the non-Living. My first work in the region
of invisible lights made me realize how in the midst
of luminous ocean we stood almost blind. Just as in
following light from visible to invisible our range of
investigation transcends our physical sight, so also
the problem of the great mystery of Life and Death is
brought a little nearer solution, when, in the realm of
the Living, we pass from the Voiced to the Unvoiced.

Sir Jagadish Chandra Bose

Ghosts

Establishing Truth about the Reality of Spirit

It may at first seem a reach to include the subject of ghosts in a book about trees. We've explored the role of trees as valued friends when solace is needed, as symbols of great ideas, as givers of energy for healing, as intermediaries between heaven and earth when a petition is tied to a branch, as dispensers of medicine when shamans contact their spirits, and on. Trees have auras, as do we all, that can be seen. They have spirits, as we do also.

Ghosts are manifestations of spirit, that when seen, help establish truth about the existence of spirit and spirit's presence. Once, I asked my healer friend Greg if he had ever seen a tree's spirit. He said, "Yes, they look something like Casper, the friendly ghost," and he sketched a little picture of an amorphous shape. The Japanese call them *kodama,* which have similar shapes.

Though I have not had the privilege of seeing a tree's spirit (so far), I actually have seen ghosts, whose existence establishes truth about the real, if unseen, world that exists around us. I'll tell you a couple of my experiences to explain.

The first time I saw a ghost was in broad daylight at my little house in Sausalito, California. A handful of people had come to meditate one afternoon, including Doug, a new attendee, of whom I knew little at the time. I led the group into meditation and soon fell into that peaceful silence that happens when the day's mind-chatter subsides. After a while I chanced to open my eyes for no particular reason, and there across the room, sitting on the couch next to Doug was a short, stocky woman with a face and hairdo I can best describe as similar to that of George Washington. She was sitting quite still with her eyes closed and seemed to be meditating. I could clearly make out her flowered dress. The pattern of the couch showed through her, because she was somewhat transparent.

I closed and opened my eyes to check a few times, but she remained there.

When the session finished I told Doug that I had seen a woman sitting beside him.

"Was she short and kind of stout, and did she look like George Washington?" he asked.

"She did! How did you know?"

"That's my mother," he said matter-of-factly. "She died years ago, and often meditates with me."

Both of these experiences came to me unbidden and unexpected, and being so, served as verifiable evidence to all the people present as witnesses, of proof that the spirit survives after death.

The second time I saw a ghost happened some months later at our weekly evening meditation group, again in my Sausalito house. There were about ten people gathered that time. It took a while for my mind to arrive at that peaceful, uncluttered silence (not always so easily attained). Before long, there gradually appeared within my inner vision the image of an auburn-haired middle-aged woman with freckles, dressed in a leotard and sitting in the yoga "lotus" position.

"Hm, nobody I know," I thought. "Could it be that I'm picking up somebody else's meditation?" Now, it is not the goal of meditation to be seeing things, but rather, to strive for and hopefully achieve peace of mind and union with God. Yet I must admit that in this altered state of consciousness it is sometimes possible to perceive other realities, or realms of existence.

I waited until everyone had shared whatever of their experiences they wished to speak about, holding back my own. But nobody spoke of the woman I saw. So at last I described my vision in as much detail as I could recall. Then Betty, who was sitting next to me leaned over and with eyes glistening, said, "Thank you, that was my aunt. She died last week. I asked her for a sign."

Both of these experiences came to me unbidden and unexpected, and being so, served as verifiable evidence to all the people present as witnesses.

But why me? Why didn't Betty see her, after all, it was her aunt? I believe it was because I just happened to be clear enough on those two occasions, to be a sort of receiving station, though unwittingly, acting, one could say, as an agent of perception. Believe me these are not common occurrences in my experience.

It is only when the working mind is temporarily put to rest that the expanded mind is free to perceive the unseen wonders all around us.

A scientist might say, "But can you repeat this at will?" for this, as we've all been taught, is the scientific method, which under most circumstances serves very well, but, we are finding, not in all circumstances. I must answer, "Nope. But that doesn't mean it didn't happen and wasn't verified."

I know those events happened. And the people who were present knew they happened too. Through my experience their faith in the continuation of the spirit was confirmed. From their experiences my own faith is strengthened.

Here's a quote I have adopted to help assess and process information, It comes from the Buddha (2,500 BCE) who said, "Believe nothing that depends only upon the authority of your masters or priests, but believe that which you yourself have tested, investigated and found reasonable, and which is for your good and that of others."

Good advice.

After Words

❧ While hiking one morning up at Phoenix Lake in Ross, California, I "heard" the voice of my friend Jan Peck urgently calling for help. But because she was living in Findhorn, Scotland, the only thing to do was trust the message and begin "sending" her help by repeating over and over, "God help Jan, God help Jan," as a sort of mantra. Within a couple of days her sister called me to say that Jan had died, alone in her room at the time I got her message. We all live only a thought away from each other.

❧ I have also seen the spirits of deceased animals and can tell you stories that would warm your heart. One was a puppy's spirit that I recognized as the same dog I had helped, but hadn't known that he died. He was happy and playful—a very reassuring vision.

❧ Here's an experiment: If you were to lie gazing up at the sky, looking into "middle distance" with your eyes just right, you could see thousands of spark-like energy particles in continuous motion crowding the air. Everything in this world is throbbing with life.

❧ You can see you own energy pretty easily by holding your hand up against a plain background. A thin, transparent aura of energy can be seen around every finger. It is called, scientifically, the "galvanic skin response."

How to Scare a Plant

Cleve Backster became world famous, but not just for being the foremost lie detector specialist in the United States. It was for what happened early in the morning of February 2, 1966, and it changed the direction of his life thereafter.

It was merely on an impulse, a whim, and out of curiosity, that he attached the electrodes of a polygraph (lie detector) to the leaf of a potted plant in his office (a dracaena, with long stem topped by long leaves). Then he watered the plant and waited to see how long it would take the water to travel up the stem to reach the leaves. He reasoned that the greater conductivity of the wetter plant would register an effect. This was recorded by a pen on the moving graph paper of the polygraph. What happened next was astounding. The plant was making human-like tracings.

Backster was now intrigued. He made a couple of gestures to get a reaction, but nothing happened. Then, wanting to maximize a reaction from the plant, he thought about what it is that makes a lie detector work on humans. Well, it turns out that the most effective way to make the lie detector react is to threaten the subject's well-being. How then, does one threaten a plant? "Burn it with a match!"

The very instant the thought crossed his mind, Backster said, "The plant went wild. The pen went off the top of the chart." (Downward means boredom; upward means alarm.)

He left the room and returned with real matches, determined to do the real deed, and see how the plant would react. Before he even struck the match there was yet another surge upward in the tracing, evidently caused by his determination to carry out the threat. It was with some reluctance that he forced himself to pass the match across a leaf. However, this time there was less reaction, indicated by a lower peak on the graph. Puzzling. He thought, "Is this plant reading my mind?"

He put the matches away to remove the threat and the plant calmed down. Later on, his lab partner repeated the experiment of intending to burn the plant to get a reaction. But when he only went through the motions of burning it without really intending to, the plant didn't react.

It appeared that the plant could differentiate between real and fake intentions. This was exciting.

In the days to follow, Backster eagerly launched into an analysis of the phenomenon, carefully eliminating one by one any other causes there might be for this effect. He could find none. He invited scientists to observe and offer explanations for his so-called thinking plants. Many suggested other possible tests, but while helpful, no one had an explanation.

One day, a Canadian botanist visited Backster, curious to witness the plant phenomenon. The plants, however, did not react for her at all. The graph showed nothing but a straight line. They seemed to have "fainted" in her presence. It was only after considerable questioning that an answer presented itself. It turned out that this researcher routinely incinerated plants for measuring dry-weight. Apparently this so alarmed Backster's plants that they simply "passed out." After the visitor left, the plants resumed normal response. It seemed that plants, like possums and praying mantises, "play dead" when faced with overwhelming danger.

The plant even registered an "alarm" response when a dog or anything else that might cause harm to the plant entered the room. One might say, in a plant's way of thinking: Moving things need watching.

Once a plant becomes attuned to its human caretaker (it takes only a drink of water) it registers definite reactions on a graph even when the caretaker is in the next room or miles away. Testing this angle, when Backster was away, his plants registered the very moment he made the decision to return home. Was it relief? Was it welcome? Giving a slide

It became apparent that plants, like opossums and praying mantises "play dead" when faced with overwhelming danger.

presentation in another city, Backster showed a picture of his hooked-up dracaena and it responded at that exact instant. He used a stopwatch and notebook to time the experiments.

He isolated the plant in a Faraday cage (a compartment that blocks electromagnetic impulses), but that didn't block the communication, eliminating electromagnetism as a factor. What seemed to be happening was more a matter of what he later termed "primary perception," having to do with a sort of "cellular consciousness." This may be the reason that plants react to the death of nearby organisms.

Furthermore, it was discovered that human interaction or involvement is not required for a plant to register reactions, which eliminated the factor of misinformation owing to human interference. The plant has its own "self" and reacts on its own.

Backster published a scientific paper in the 1968 *International Journal of Parapsychology* titled "Evidence of Primary Perception in Plant Life." The information was now available for other scientists to make their own experiments. The response was enormous. Seven thousand scientists requested reprints. Using the basic traditional scientific method of repeatability, they experimented. While it worked sometimes, at other times it didn't. Missing was the "spontaneity" factor that Backster found to be all-important. But the use of spontaneity as a tool for measuring scientific experiments is not permissible in the traditional laboratory.

The study was also time consuming and tedious. "You can't get plants to just jump through a hoop ten times in a row." Backster had his supporters, but not enough to silence the hisses of ridicule from other scientists' failed experiments.

"Spontaneity versus repeatability is what has held back the scientific community for years," says Backster. It was maddening; the necessary planning of a lab experiment almost ensures its failure in the area of exploring consciousness. To ensure repeatability, it's got to be totally automated to remove all human consciousness (and therefore the attitude or expectations of the experimenter). In other words, you would just go about your other business, ignoring the plant, and check on it later.

If Backster's discovery proved valid, major adjustments to accepted models of science would be required. The resulting threat to respected reputations and to well-upholstered egos would only make the going a whole lot tougher. Just imagine having to change all those textbooks, for instance.

You can't get plants to just jump through a hoop ten times in a row.

How to Scare a Plant

Buddhist and Hindu scientists, when presented with Backster's information say, "What took you so long?"

So what has happened in the years since? How has Western science dealt with this troublesome, irritating problem? While some people have declared the research a "life-changing event," most do what always works: ignore or ridicule it.

Buddhist and Hindu scientists when presented with Backster's information say, "What took you so long?"

Backster says, "'The Gaia hypothesis' (that earth is a working organism with its own corrections built in) fits well with my work. . . . and I strongly feel that nature has its ways of handling abuse."

After Words

- ❦ Plants were only the beginning; Cleve Backster's work with yogurt, bacteria, food, and human cells has been a crowning achievement in his ongoing work.

- ❦ There are stories about the axe-man begging a tree's forgiveness before felling it. Well, now there is plenty of evidence to support that quaint notion. It is a fact that an oak tree actually "quakes" or "quivers" at the approach of an axe-man.

- ❦ Rupert Sheldrake, the research scientist, rigged up time-action cameras on both a dog at home alone and on its human at work. At the moment that the human thought of heading for home, his dog trotted over to the door expectantly. Habit was not a factor since the experiment required the human's actions to be spontaneous and occurs at random times.

- ❦ Back when I lived in my Sausalito house, I let Tim, a kid traveling alone and out of money, bunk in my studio. He later sent a card of thanks, but no return address. I put the card aside on my "wait and see" pile. Two years later, cleaning out old stuff, I found the card. Holding it, I thought, "I'd love to know how you're getting on, Tim. Send me your address please."

    Within five days I received a letter from Tim saying, "I don't really know why I'm writing this since I'm fine and doing well. . . ." He included his return address both at the close of the letter and on the envelope. Moreover, he was writing from Connecticut, on the East Coast, to me in California, on the West Coast, some 3,000 miles away. This meant that he had "received" my thought at about the moment I "sent" it. This, to me, is proof that time and space have no bearing on our communications with one another.

    We are all connected: plants, animals, and each other; I know this for a fact.

- ❦ "No man is an island, entire of itself; every man is a piece of the continent, a part of the main," says the seventeenth-century poet John Donne. And a plant is too.

The ideal chemist of the future will not be
satisfied with humdrum day-to-day analysis,
but is one who dares to think with an
independence not permissible heretofore . . .

George Washington Carver
An agricultural chemist who spoke with plants
and saw their spirits (1860–1943)

Observations

Confessions

All right, I admit it, I prune plants. Gardeners do. Pinching, pulling and pruning are all part of the job description. That's just how it is, and we don't think of ourselves as torturers, though Cleve Backster's polygraphed plants would no doubt disagree. Where is the cutoff point, so to speak, between an acceptable and unacceptable snip of the old aspidistra? Must we forgo the satisfaction of admiring our well-clipped hedges? See there, how the sunlight glides across the shorn surfaces, see how beautifully the smooth planes define space, how ordered the landscape becomes as we prune away the chaos and confusion of competitive vegetation, creating an organized little world of our own making. It fools us into thinking that we're actually in charge for awhile.

The Garden of Eden was probably a tangled mess before Adam and Eve took it over and started pinching and rearranging things. They started it. It was their willfulness that got us into the mess we've been in ever since because they just couldn't keep their hands off those trees. But I like the sweet notion that it was in a garden that time, as some measure it, began.

And so lovely are the ordered rows of well-tended orchards and vineyards, or the carefully raked pebbles in a Japanese garden, combed to remind us of the sea, encircling great stones, chosen to remind us of islands or mountains—the universe on a small, manageable scale.

. . . a Japanese garden, combed to remind us of the sea, encircling great stones, chosen to remind us of islands or mountains— the universe on a small, manageable scale.

Though chaos runs wild beyond the walls, within, the garden is controlled and safe.

Adding to this pruning dilemma, there is a highly prized plant art called Bonsai, the miniaturization of otherwise large trees by methodically pruning their roots and limbs. The resulting tiny trees are amazingly exact in every minute detail. The leaves of a maple tree pruned in this way are exquisite, perfectly formed replicas of their normal-size parents. How perfectly they fit into the Japanese garden universe: nature as art.

Followers of the ancient Jaina sect of India no doubt throw their hands up in despair at this barbaric practice. If the Jainas had a motto it would be, "Do No Harm," like the physicians' Hippocratic oath. The Jainas, ever watchful that they cause no inconvenience to their fellow beings of whatever kingdom, from smallest to mightiest, regard the whole cosmos as alive and therefore capable of suffering injury.

To injure, they say, would be to "stain the subtle crystal of one's life-monad." And though we're mystified as to the exact meaning of this phrase, we know we don't want that to happen. A dictionary definition of *monad* is "an indivisible, indestructible unit that is the basic element of reality, and a microcosm of it." The Big Purpose at the root of this rather extreme belief is to escape from the endless rounds of reincarnations on this earth, caused by our offense against even the smallest of others. The Jainas' desire is to exit this earth plane, never to return, and move on to worthier pursuits in the vast universe.

Now although I appreciate this deeply earnest belief, it seems to me that the physical world is doing everything it possibly can to block the exits. Life abounds. Life crams the corridors. Growth is irresistible, unstoppable, and what you prune grows back.

Therefore, practical solutions must be found for this business of doing no harm. We just can't help bumping into or trampling on something or "somebody" at every turn, much as we try to avoid doing so. Mindful of the danger of staining the subtle crystal of my "life-monad," ever darkening with accumulated karma (debts owed and rewards earned), I vote for a respectful middle path, while making sure there are wild nature preserves set aside, untouched by human hands.

So my pruning shears shall stay sharpened a while longer. The clipped boxwood organizing my personal little garden universe must remain shorn. It's their fate and my need, and that, for the time being, is that.

However, there is one thing we can do, a simple offering that we can make to the Jainas among us, a small glint of light to brighten the crystals of all our life-monads. Here it is: Plant things that don't require much

pruning. After much thought, I'm heading in that direction myself, to a chorus of sighs from my relieved plants.

For instance, if you want a column, you could plant glauca cypress, whose nature it is to grow that way; or instead of grass, plant a low-growing ground cover; or substitute dwarf English boxwood and dwarf English lavender in a formal garden: They require less pruning, thus leaving more time for you to luxuriate in your chaise longue, admiring the results.

Winter gales act as nature's clean-out system, by blowing down dead and rotting branches that harbor invasive bugs. Taking nature's lead, we can groom trees, too, being mindful of habitats before we start sawing. I was about to cut a dead, hole-pocked oak branch only to discover that it was home to a clan of entertaining, acrobatic chickadees. They help groom their trees by eating bugs. So do woodpeckers eat bugs, and they need dead trees as living quarters to base their insect-hunting expeditions. Aren't a few beautifully dressed woodpeckers preferable to poisonous insect sprays? My friends Norman and Shelly at Arrowsmith Farm solved their bug problem with ducks that patrol the rows, muttering softly as they go.

I was about to cut a dead, hole-pocked oak branch only to discover that it was home to a clan of entertaining, acrobatic chickadees.

Shamans, the original experts, say that trees and plants are very forgiving and have a lot of forbearance. Trees are even willing to cooperate with humans if we would just develop a little common courtesy. Asking permission isn't so hard if we regard plants as fellow beings engaged as we all are in the intricate dance of life. One should address them with the respect due to every living thing. We'll know when it feels right, they tell us. "Be natural."

After Words

 Voltaire's message in *Candide* goes something like this: After the trials, tribulations, affronts, and injustices in life have been endured, in the end it is enough to tend our fields, live our lives, and make our gardens grow.

 I heard a Maori healer of New Zealand say, "Our Tahuna told us to always have respect for the trees we harvest medicine from. When you take leaves, always take them from the east side of a tree, the side the sun blesses first thing in the morning. It will heal faster. And take only enough leaves to fill the hand. Remember to give a few back to Tane, the forest god, and dedicate the leaves to him."

The task of gathering medicine from a tree requires a focused spirit; this is what guides a person to the right plant for the condition they wish to heal. The plant will tell you its properties.

❦ At my nursery's growing grounds, the staff no longer tightly stakes their trees, but allows slack for back-and-forth wind movement. The resistance makes the trunks grow stronger. Ross, the boss, told me that the movement breaks, then reheals the plants cells, which then heal faster as they become accustomed to the stress. So, overcoming a little stress does actually make us stronger. But we knew that. My nursery plays music for the plants too.

The Tree Connection

Plants live and die, enjoy health, and suffer disease, just as we do. They grow, "bleed," sleep, awaken, and renew. So we can relate to them and take comfort in their recurring cycles, because we experience life in similar ways. But what's more, plants have spirits as we do.

> *. . . all mankind can learn to accept and*
> *listen to the voices of Nature.*
> *We can learn to reconnect ourselves with*
> *the spiritual essence of the universe.*

Harold Kramer, Publisher
(from the Preface of
Talking with Nature by M. J. Roads)

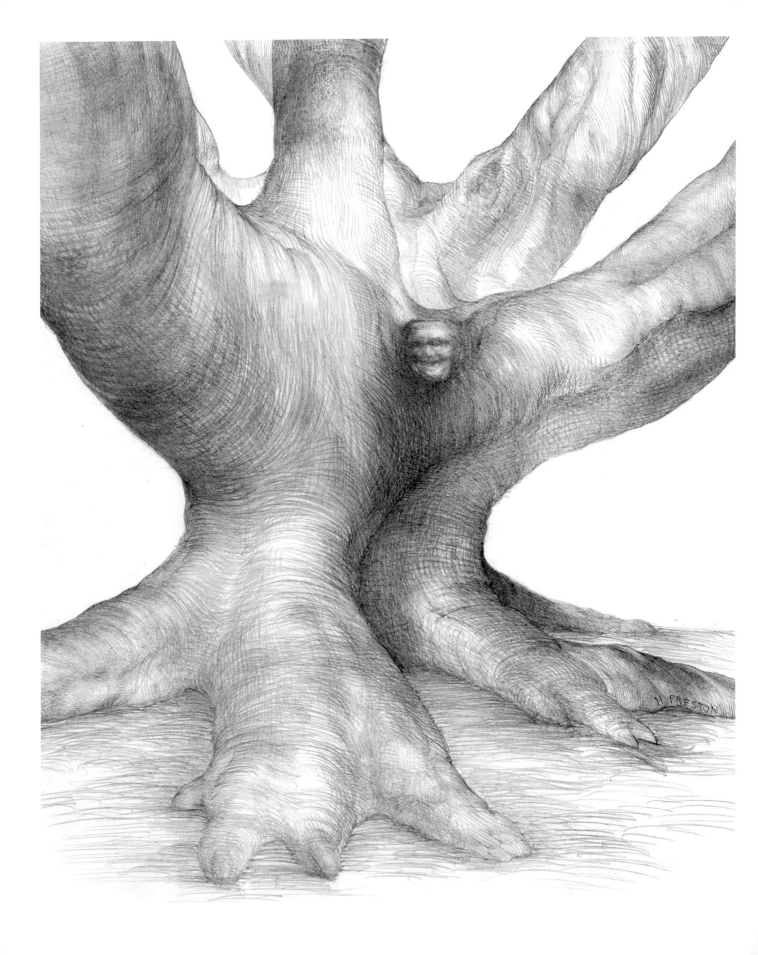

The Great Madrone

We came upon it suddenly one day when Janet and I were hiking over a remote wooded ridge above Fairfax, California. We stopped dead in our tracks. "Wow! Look at that," we said. There, not 20 feet off the narrow path, partially hidden by rabbit brush, loomed the most enormous madrone tree we had ever seen or imagined existed. Parting the brush, we slowly entered the circular clearing, approaching the tree as though to a castle, ourselves as vassals coming to pay homage to a powerful ruler.

Six gigantic, solid, sinewy limbs reached out in every direction, their immense strength defying gravity's pull. Healed scars showed evidence of other limbs long since gone. The tree's stance was like that of a muscled wrestler's, and its thick, red roots like dragon's feet, claws puncturing and disappearing into the earth.

Our hands were all over it, stroking its mighty trunk. Its surface was mostly smooth where the bark sloughed off into nakedness, with ripples and creases like human skin but hard, very hard. Its color was mottled peach with gray and rust red here and there. In the uppermost branches, some large, leathery leaves, caught in a passing breeze flapped against the sky. The paper-thin bark looked exactly like small gray scales,

The impression it gave was of a wise and very old sage with an expression of bemused benevolence.

thousands of them the size of thumbnails all arranged in orderly lines, like the armored mail-plates of medieval warriors.

Then we saw the face. It was astonishing. Protruding from the intersection of its lower trunk was a perfectly formed, life-sized face. If ever a tree manifested its guardian spirit from within its being, this was it. Its two eye sockets were complete with eyes, eyelids, and brow ridge. Its nose was flat but delineated, like a jack-o'-lantern's. The mouth was wide, the smile a little crooked, like Houdin's sculpture of Voltaire, and the teeth a bit snaggled. But the creased and swelling cheeks were charmingly dimpled, the chin firm and jaunty. There was even a "hairline" above the brow. The impression it gave was of a wise and very old sage with an expression of bemused benevolence.

The knot from which this face grew fell within a slightly bluish strain between the jutting limbs that cradled it. This set apart even more, the face from its host. The effect was startling. We looked for evidence of tampering but found none.

We gauged that several men could stand around its trunk, arms outstretched, fingers touching, that is if they squatted, duck-fashion. "Let's measure it," I said.

Now the dendrologist's rule for measuring the size of trees for comparison purposes is to take the tree's circumference 4 feet from the ground. But since the lowest branches interrupted that measure, and the madrone's "waist" was below 3 feet, we would have to improvise and compromise. We agreed on a procedure: One of us would reach our arms from a marked starting point on the trunk; then the other would put a finger on the next point and reach around to the next until arriving again at the starting point. This roughly approximated what a tape measure would have given us. "Thirty-four feet!" we said together.

When we did finally return with proper tools, the final count was 34 feet 8 inches. And as it was a vigorous tree still growing, who knows what girth it would yet attain.

I'll always be grateful that we returned, not only with measuring tape, but camera and film enough to preserve a record of the old fellow in that stage of his life. For over the years time and the elements have taken their toll. One by one the old sage's features have fallen away, a reminder of our own mortality. As mythologist Joseph Campbell philosophically said of his own aging, "There goes a headlight, there goes a fender."

From time to time we have returned to pay our respects to the old madrone, always sensing in its presence a quiet regard that those who go there feel for it, except for a few thoughtless markings. I like to think of it as the restraint of respect.

Yesterday I hiked back for a visit, my steps accompanied by a sense of eagerness mixed with foreboding. To my utter dismay, the tree's fallen remains were spread in ruins across the earth. I sighed, made my way in, stroked the old fellow, then sat at its base to mourn its passing. Finally I crawled over and around the litter. Then I found them. Two new green branches sprouting from the splintered trunk. A reprieve! A last surge from its staunch undaunted spirit, triumphing over a premature death, refusing to be finished.

"It came down in our last big winter storm. Too many feet tamping down the vulnerable soil beneath it for too many years," said Jonathan, our Open Space advocate, later. Ranger Casey said, "It was loved to death."

As I write, the leathery leaves, once unreachable at tree-top, are now within reach beside my drawing board in a glass of water, along with a younger madrone's white spring flowers, filling the studio with their musty, honeyed fragrance, and a promise of continuance.

Yesterday I hiked back for a visit, my steps accompanied by a sense of eagerness mixed with foreboding.

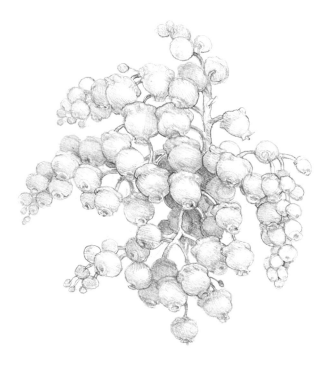

The Small Madrone

There was a small madrone tree living on our newly acquired land. But it intruded into an overgrown, rarely used, though potentially useful pathway. The tree was five and a half feet tall like myself, a bit straggly, a bit like my gardener-self, but with lovely smooth, peach skin, exactly like mine, well, sort of. But it also had beautiful, large, green, oval leaves fanning from long, twiggy branches, and bright, hard, red berry clusters. Otherwise, we were almost an even match. I use these comparisons, as you shall see.

This will make a fine pathway one of these days, I thought. With a snip here and a pinch there, I could coax this tree to grow upwards instead of sideways, so I thought. I thus proceeded to prune it as I would any other tree, with the same expectations of compliance. So I began heading back the unwanted buds and branchlets to encourage growth in the direction I wanted it to grow. The madrone, however, refused to cooperate, continuing to grow sideways. This behavior, in my experience was decidedly odd. Yet I kept on snipping and pinching.

As season followed season, my expectations were met with disappointment; my patience was giving way to frustration. I stubbornly persisted with my pruning strategy; however, the more I persisted, the more it resisted. Be patient, I told myself.

Occasionally, as I walked down to what I had begun to regard as the battleground to check its progress, there would be only the tiniest indication of a green bud, out to the side, of course, nowhere else. This was not good. After all, this plant-retraining process takes a lot of time and patience, and I was about out of both.

"I am at war with a plant," I grimly admitted. "And it is winning."

My next visit to the battleground was without results of any kind. "This is the most uncooperative, obstinate, spiteful plant I have ever met. And now it refuses to put out even a single leaf. This is too much. And besides, it's a very poor specimen of a madrone at that." I gave it more water. Still it refused to cooperate.

Had I known better, or had I simply paid the least attention to the obvious, I'd have understood that it had its own intentions, which was what it was already doing: growing sideways. Also, I was getting the distinct feeling that this tree did not like people in general, and me in particular, which made me very uncomfortable.

Another season passed. Nothing. Stalemate. Then I became aware of a sort of lethargy about the little tree, a retreat from the battle. Not a surrender. That would have been undignified. It was more like a decision to quit, as if to say, "What's the use?" For some reason that I couldn't name, I felt uneasy as I left it to do other things.

It was some time before I again trod down the path to see how things were. "Oh!" I cried aloud. A sense of profound loss and despair swept over me when I gazed at the little madrone. It had lost all of its beautiful leaves and berries. Its branches were bare, skeletal, shriveled, its color darkened. Dead.

Finally I understood. I was deeply sad. It was entirely my fault. Why couldn't I just leave it alone? Hadn't I seen that it wasn't like other trees? It was a loner, like me, and I couldn't leave it alone. It was a hard lesson I learned that day.

After Words

❦   In the foothills of the Sierra Nevada mountains an old fellow says of madrones, "They don't like people messing with 'em. Leave 'em alone and maybe they'll grow and maybe they won't."

❦ My local nursery doesn't sell madrones. Tom and Ross, the nurserymen say, "They don't like containers. They don't like sitting in water. They don't like runoff from other plants. So they're hard to care for. They naturally grow in scrubland. They're very slow growers so that they can conserve their energy. They're just too darned temperamental. And they're hard to grow. So we won't carry them."

❦ Sunset's *Western Garden* book says: "If you live in madrone country and you have a madrone tree in your garden, treasure it . . . its requirements are exacting!" Amen.

❦ My friend Gay's nurseryman told her not to make loud noises around her madrone because, he insists, noise alarms them.

Oaks, Rock Devas, and a Tree Goddess

Contributed by Michael and Justine Toms, Co-founders of New Dimensions World Broadcasting Network

A Friend Saved

Two magnificent oaks live by our home in Mendocino County, California. They have been here since the indigenous people of this valley gathered acorns under its branches for food. These trees continue to provide sustenance for countless critters, and a glory of birds. These old trees still speak to us every day, even though we thought we'd lose one when the local arborist told us that it should be taken down. But we cried, "No!"

Thereafter, we ritually embraced that tree and told it we wanted it to live long, and that we would give it all the support it needed. Much to our delight it is still alive, well, and happily, providing its yearly offering of acorn offspring.

Barn or Tree

There's another oak, in the bayou country of Louisiana, on the farm of Justine's paternal great, great, great grandfather. As we stood under the arms of that massive grandmother oak planted by her ancestor 160 years before, this is the story we were told: the tree was planted beside the original barn, but by and by after many years, the tree began to press against the barn's roof threatening to cave it in. So what was he to do, cut the tree down? No sir, he moved the barn!

Now the barn is gone, and only the tree remains. But in that tree is carried the energetic of her family roots, communicating in a way that is beyond all words.

Devas

We once lived in an old mineral-springs resort on Duncan Peak outside of Hopland, California. It had 88 acres of rustic land with varieties of oaks. Forced by circumstances, we put the land up for sale. But during that final year we were deeply blessed by the land and all the life residing upon it; wildlife showed up that hadn't been in evidence in any of the previous four years. And Rock Devas showed themselves to us.

One day as we walked by the stream that ran through the land, the dark tree goddess, protector of the mountain, was shown to us. We caught our breath, both feeling that it was the spirit of the land gifting us with her presence.

She revealed herself through a fortuitous "accident" when Michael tripped and fell down into a soft depression of leaves by the creek. In the excitement Justine ran down to join Michael delightedly rolling in the leaves, luxuriating in the thrill of being held by mother earth. Lying, gazing up at the deep blue sky through the dense foliage, suddenly a hummingbird flew in, pausing directly over Michael in such a way as to direct his attention to the sacred tree. She was an ancient oak transformed by lightning as if by the hands of a renaissance sculptor who had carved her flowing robes and dark face.

We were awestruck. Why hadn't we ever seen her before?

Now we understand that before such mysteries can be revealed, one needs to have humility of mind and body. We were filled with gratitude.

It is only through a change in human consciousness that the world will be transformed.

The personal and the planetary are connected. As we expand our awareness of body, mind, psyche and spirit, so also will the world be changed. This is our quest as we explore new dimensions.

From the "New Dimensions" opening theme

Where the House God Lives

Some years ago I acquired a handsome old Shinto house-shrine as a decorative work of art. A Japanese craftsman built it of pine in about 1850 to resemble the ancient temples of Japan. It has two little pillars flanking seven steps leading to double doors opening into a sanctuary within. Its elegant, overhanging roof is elaborately carved and characteristically curved upward.

I placed it near the central pillar of our house. It seemed the correct location though I did not then know why. I wrote a blessing for our home on a small piece of paper and put it inside the little shrine because it seemed the right thing to do. This is where it has stayed ever since, protected and protective. Over the years this little shrine has added a sense of peace and beauty to our lives, an architectural grace, a connection to a mysterious past, and a reminder of the unseen world around us.

Yet compared with Japan's ancient Shinto shrine of Ise (ee-say, 260 CE) it is a mere echo. The real temple dwells serenely in its sacred cedar grove on a peninsula jutting into the Pacific Ocean; its unexcelled architecture is a breathtaking expression of sublime simplicity.

Hidden within its deepest recesses are three Sacred Treasures: the sacred beads, the sacred sword, and the sacred mirror that no eye has ever seen, wrapped in cloth layers then tucked in brocade bags. But though these material treasures are famous and excite the imagination, there is another object, a humble treasure of even more importance.

It stands below the temple's raised floor exactly in the center and contains magical power that from its outward appearance no one would suspect. It is a simple, round, freestanding wooden post, about 5 feet high, called the "heart pillar." It is of no structural use whatsoever, yet it is the most valuable object in the entire shrine. Its sole purpose is to provide a place for the nature gods to reside. Through this post the gods descend to earth.

The post represents its long-gone sacred tree. Trees were known as pathways for the gods, a *yorishiro.* For does not lightning striking a tree prove that trees are pathways for the gods? It has always been so. In another location, the Izumo shrine, the pillar is called "the esteemed pillar of the heart."

Shinto means the way of the *kami* "spirit" or teaching of the nature gods. Shinto belief honors the divinity of trees. Deep in time's silent shadows, even before the mythological Age of the Gods who were giants then, Shinto worshipped nature, offering gratitude to the beneficent forces of nature.

One might need to appease a malevolent force from time to time, but being thankful was more important than being fearful. Both the material world and the spiritual world were regarded as equals, neither was superior to the other. Plants, rocks, birds, beasts, fishes, water, sun, moon, earthquakes, thunder, all the heavenly and earthly forces were objects of reverence and respect. Shinto has no founder since it evolved from pre-history, no sacred scriptures, and no dogma.

Shinto was hijacked and altered for political purposes a while before World War II. But it has been mostly restored to its purer form and respectfully survives today. Now this is a belief that's easy to appreciate.

In old Japanese households the god of the house still lives in the central pillar. There is a New Year's custom in which pine branches and a rope of straw are attached to the pillar. Offerings of pounded rice and rice wine are reverently placed before it. Children are cautioned not to lean against the central pillar since this would show disrespect for the place where the god *kami* lives. Now there's a concept we might adopt, if only to keep the word "respect" in our lives.

Shinto belief honors the divinity of trees. Deep in time's silent shadows, even before the mythological Age of the Gods who were giants then, Shinto worshipped nature, offering gratitude to the beneficent forces of nature

In some Japanese houses the symbolic tree-pillar takes on breathtaking proportions as an architectural feature, a visual inspiration. Whole tree trunks have even been used to this purpose, their branches spiraling up and out to support beams high overhead. Until I find such a tree for my central pillar I content myself, in the spirit of simplicity, with the symbol: a tree where the house god lives.

The house god of my little Shinto shrine, though felt, remains unrevealed. But the structural pillar beside it holding the roof seems just right. I've always thought of the wood pillars in our house as representing trees, the walls merely as weather-guards, and the windows as vistas to the real world of nature outside. Now it all seems fitting.

After Words

- The Ise shrine has been dismantled and totally rebuilt every 20 years since the late 600's CE (except during periods of military unrest.) Visiting Ise, I found the shrine protected from outsiders by four concentric fences. I just managed a glimpse inside by tiptoe. It is still a place of reverence and pilgrimage as the spiritual home of the Japanese people. The August Mirror is the symbol of the *kami* residing in the inner sanctum. It is sacred to the sun goddess. Food and textiles are offered.

- When approaching the altar, one makes two deep bows, followed by two handclaps, followed by two more bows. (This gets the attention of the kami, who are probably otherwise occupied.)

- Throughout Japan there are consecrated rocks and evergreen trees where *kami* reside.

- To show that a sacred tree is revered and to sanctify it, a sacred rope, *shiminawa,* is tied around it like a belt. No evil can pass beyond the line of this rope. The *shiminawa* is made of two strands of rice straw plaited together, one representing positivity, the other negativity: opposites from which all nature was formed. A few rice stalks are hung from the rope at intervals. These woven ropes are hung above gates, around shrines and in other sacred places. The temple ropes are enormous.

- George Nakashima, master woodworker, believed that trees have souls. In his woodwork he tried to bring out those souls rather than treat the wood as just so much raw material. (Eberling 1998)

- It is told that the man who made legendary baseball bats wandered out through a forest in search of a tree whose soul matched the soul of the batter.

- Our friends at Arrowsmith Farm recommended a feng shue (fung shway) expert to examine our house to see if the *chi* (universal energy) was flowing properly. Happily, it was; and what's more, we harbored a guardian spirit, a sort of angel. Of course, we knew this already since, in a poetic moment, we had invited one to come watch over things. I like thinking that our Shinto shrine is exactly its appropriate residence.

George Nakashima, master woodworker, believed that trees have souls. In his woodwork he tried to bring out those souls rather than treat the wood as just so much raw material.

Where the House God Lives

The Oldest Tree on Earth

The temperature hit 120 degrees crossing Death Valley that late spring afternoon. Following the sun in slow-fall, burning a sky trail, we headed westward towards the shadowed hills. Furnace-hot air scorched my arm and sucked my lungs dry when I lowered the car window. But this harsh, parched land has an undeniable if unforgiving beauty, even when seen through baked eyes.

Eager to be leaving this lowest place on the North American continent, we headed northwest towards the continent's highest point, Mount Whitney, only eighty miles away. I counted contrasts. Easy to do. We'd come from a wedding in Las Vegas, Nevada, that most synthetic of towns, where in casinos nothing is real but the yearnings of gamblers staring spellbound at clanging machines in timeless, eternal twilight.

We had passed abruptly from the town limits into barren, rock-strewn hills on the last stretch of our journey and my personal pilgrimage. I was on a treasure hunt. We were going to hunt down the oldest living tree on earth just hours ahead, hidden within the White Mountains of California. I could barely contain myself.

The welcomed tranquility and green loveliness of the Owens River valley lay sheltered at the feet of the high White Mountains. The town of Bishop with its rustling cottonwoods would be our resting place and starting point for the 10,000-foot climb up the mountains next morning. I gazed at the high crest concealing the ancient one's dwelling place. My heart beat faster.

Next morning we dutifully packed the car with the warm clothing, hiking gear, plenty of water, and the trail food the information brochure said we'd need for the subsequent four-and-a-half-mile trek in the thin, cold air up beyond the ranger station. I'd had nosebleeds at lower altitudes.

The rounded, fawn-colored foothills resembled deer cuddled against the higher mid-range hills, covered with little gray-green porcupine-like sages that feel silky when touched and that appear to be scuttling in arrested motion up the mountain.

As we approached the summit, the views were spectacular. To the west the jagged Sierra Nevada mountains gleamed white with snow; to the south Death Valley baked away; while below and northward the green Owens valley nested serenely, separating the two mountain ranges.

Then fortune frowned. At the juncture, the gravel road to the largest bristlecones in the Patriarch grove was closed, unpassable because of snow. Yet in truth it was not the biggest tree I wanted to see; it was the oldest that excited me. So we turned toward the Methuselah grove, parked, and hauled out our gear.

More bad luck. The ranger station was closed. No guide books, no expert, and no trail map. We peered in the window to see what we were missing, read some explanatory signs, then quietly looked at each other, shrugged, and started down the steep, gravelly mountain trail. The barren slopes are of white alkaline dolomite limestone, looking like bleached heaps of broken teeth. They clinked as we tread on them. We would need to step carefully and pace ourselves for the next four and a half miles. The high altitude made breathing a strain.

Almost immediately we were surrounded by vast tribes of wizened old bristlecone pines, sparsely covering the slopes, above and below the trail for miles everywhere we looked, hundreds and hundreds of them. We were already walking among trees that might be 3,000 and 4,000 years old. But the one I was in search of had been in existence for nearly 5,000 years . . . Yes, that old! It is called Methuselah (after the oldest man in the Bible who lived a mere 969 years). And it still lived somewhere in the vicinity of this very path. How could it have survived all those years?

It is rumored that a bristlecone exists that is even older than the Methuselah, but only the anointed know where it is, and they are sworn to secrecy. I'll explain later . . . but first let's get some perspective on this age thing. I stopped to consider what we were experiencing here, and pondered what was happening in human history 5,000 years ago. In Egypt the pyramids were being built. The Minoan culture on Crete was barely emerging, China's Bronze Age wouldn't appear for another thousand years. Buddha wouldn't be born for about another 2,300 years, or Jesus for 3,000, or Mohammed for 4,430. All the recorded history we thought was so important hadn't happened yet. But on a remote mountain in California a little green bristlecone sprout called Methuselah sprang to life.

On this same mountain the wind softly sighed. As we passed, a pinecone dropped and rolled to the drift below its ancient parent tree as we passed. A crow sailed from a bristlecone, cawing, nutcrackers scolded a ground squirrel, bees hummed, and we spied tracks in the last of a shrinking snowfield. But except for these rare sounds and the rising of a wind-tone chorus blowing over the mountain heights and droning down through ancient branches, the bristlecones live in peaceful silence.

These pines brim with sap, as I soon discovered when stroking a long, green, foxtail of a branch. The sticky, fragrant pitch scented my fingers for hours. I kept sniffing it and stroked another branch later to prolong the heady perfume. The sap helps preserve them. The little bristled spikes on their cones gave them their name.

When a dendrologist drills a pencil thin hole into a bristlecone's core to determine its age, the hole rapidly fills with sap, plugging it again. In counting the number of growth rings, one ring equals one year. Wide rings show rainy years, tight rings, drought. Since bristlecones grow very slowly the wood is exceedingly dense and hard. The history of the earth for almost 11,000 years can be read through a method called cross-counting, which is a careful overlapping of matching rings from trees of different ages. Even long dead trees can be cored and counted since the wood takes so long to finally disintegrate.

The results are extremely accurate, and when coordinated with archeological digs and known historic events, this method for dating trees is more reliable than carbon-14 dating. So rain and floods, fire and ash from volcanic eruptions, droughts and climate changes leave a clear, secret record inside trees. And because of the bristlecone's unusual habitat and long life they are the best record keepers.

Astoundingly, according to the U.S. Forest Service, fallen remains "have been found intact with tree rings that are 9,000+ years old."

The Oldest Tree on Earth

So, okay, did I connect with a bristlecone spirit? Whether or not it was their immense age that intimidated me, or my lack of more finely attuned sensibilities, the truth is, I simply couldn't "reach" their spirit. I was too engrossed and distracted by their beautiful, convoluted forms, thrilling to the artist's eye. Let me tell you, they are absolutely fantastic: twisting, curling, corkscrewing from eons of wind erosion and sandblasting, sometimes imitating gray rock forms or dried honey. Their trunks ripple, and striate. Some, their limbs like candelabrum, stand frozen in stark, startled eternity. Others look like stop-frame explosions.

What did I feel about the ancient trees I met? I simply found them patiently involved with the process of re-creating life from themselves, uninterested, unconcerned, indifferent to what we short-lived human gnats think. Just leave them alone, and they will mark the ages at their own contented pace. They will continue to draw just enough nurture from the earth and sky to form narrow bands of living bark snaking up the scarcely living trunk or on long-dead limbs, to feed their branches and neat green needles; then to make cones of male and female, and from the cones, drop winged seeds into the waiting earth. That is enough.

Well, what about Methuselah? Did we meet the Methuselah tree? Ah, it was "hidden" somewhere in plain sight to save its life from vandals, unmarked, anonymous. Alas.

We completed the circle trek in early evening, breathing hard, bodies tired, but heads swimming with lingering visions and the faint, retreating roar of ancient eons echoing in our ears. There would be time enough later to regard the lost meeting with Methuselah in philosophical forbearance, but for now we felt gratified in every cell to have come. I didn't wash my hand that night.

After Words

❧ The bristlecones survive so long not in spite of, but because of their harsh, hostile environment. The steep, barren slopes they cling to have very little nutrient value. Other plants shun it. So the bristlecones have little competition. Gale-force winds rip over the crests and down the canyons. Subzero winter temperatures batter them almost to ruins, and their yearly growing season lasts only about six weeks. They have devised severe survival techniques for severe conditions. Live bark will sprout new growth when better times and conditions come around again. What's a couple of hundred years to a bristlecone?

❧ A bristlecone can hang onto its needles for forty years. Its boney root system is enormous, making up 90 percent of the tree's total mass. But they don't rise much higher than 35 feet, 50 feet at most. Water is scarce. Stunningly, the oldest trees that have endured and survived the lonely ages are the ones most deprived, while bristlecones getting adequate water don't live as long.

❦ **Get ready here it comes:** In 1964, the mountain's silence was shattered by the sound of a chain saw wielded by a graduate science student named Donald whose coring drill had broken when he was drilling a particularly decrepit tree in order to determine its age. He asked for and was given permission from the Forestry Service to cut it down so he could count its rings. He was in a hurry, after all, wasn't he? Keith Trexler, a forest ranger, was assigned to observe.

It took about five guys to fell and slice it clean enough to see its rings. Donald hauled a few choice slices down the mountain for further polishing. It took him a week with a magnifying glass to count 4,900 rings and discover that he had killed the oldest living tree on earth. Years later when asked if he had any twinges of remorse about the deed back then, he said, "No, but I do now." (Unknown to him, admirers had previously named it Prometheus: the god who gave fire to mortals.)

So, that is why the really old ones are kept secret now. Vandals do it for sport, scientists, for Science.

❦ **A stunning "coincidence:"** Four years after writing this essay, I started drawing its accompanying bristlecone illustration when my friend Diane Richard called, asking what I was working on. I told her the story I've just told you. She was touched by the cutting death of Prometheus, and subsequently told the story to her friend Kris Trexler, who said, "But I know all about it; my husband Keith was a National Park Service Naturalist assigned to observe. He took the only pictures of Prometheus before and after it was cut down, and I have the pictures as well as some of its wood!" It turned out she now lives only thirty minutes from my home—after 45 years living in many distant places! So I introduced myself by email and was graciously invited to come see, which I eagerly did. I held a wood fragment from that ancient tree and then took photographs, the only pictures of the oldest tree on Earth. Boggling.

Why the Change

When trees, once intensely worshiped, become regarded as mere matter or just so many board feet of lumber, a profound change has taken place in human consciousness. Something held to be precious has been lost. The sacred trees are no longer viewed as living, conscious beings with spirits of their own. The voice and vital hum of life inherent in all things from rocks and streams to air and trees is silenced, soulless. We have bypassed the tree's own spirit but seized its celebrity, replacing it with flashy gods in human form. In J. G. Frazer's words, "freed, or disengaged from each particular tree, tree spirits begin to change shape and assume the body of a man."

Skillfully sculpted statues of athletic heroes and heroines, some imaginatively sprouting branches or wearing leafy garments, substitute for what was once a real tree spirit.

So guess who has the power now? The power transfers to a man-god imbued with supernatural powers, an idol. He has taken over the power the tree once had to make the sun to shine, the rain to fall, flocks to multiply, and women to give safe birth. Then what happened, says Fraser, was that "the very same powers became incarnate in *living* men." Think of Diana's enthronement of the living man, Verbius, as first King of the Woods.

When a tree spirit becomes only a symbol and that symbol is in human form, the symbol becomes an idol. The idol as an object then gets

worshiped. Wise ones of old have warned against the worship of idols. Here might be a good example.

When the tree spirit is nudged aside, we are free to regard the tree as we like. Well, almost. Even unrecognized, that spirit still exists with its own specific function in nature's vast system.

But psychics tell us that the full vitality nature needs to perform its rightful functions is somehow diminished when we turn our backs on the unseen world around us. Without feeling the respect and love from which all of us thrive, nature spirits can get by, but only just. Dr. Rudolf Steiner said our not recognizing the unseen deprives them of some spiritual nourishment. The Balinese musicians asked, "Where are your tree spirits?"

When the tree loses its position of power and is no longer regarded as important, it becomes compromised, minimized, trivialized, and eventually ignored. Sadly, that's where we find ourselves today. Our ancient reverence for trees, born of conviction from our experiences, gradually became degraded into ignorant, fearful superstition.

And so, little by little, as we questioned the old beliefs, the power of trees dribbled down into the careless hands of modern man, greatly diminished, devoid of richness, bereft of meaning, and lacking spirit.

Having lost their power to save themselves, trees are now in service to us. And who but we moderns would cut down a beautiful tree to splinter into toothpicks?

A Pitch for Animism, or Let's Hear It for Spirit

First came animism, the belief that all things in nature have souls or consciousness; then came polytheism, the worship of many gods, each representing this or that aspect of nature's various forces, Neptune as god of the sea, for instance. And so on we "progressed" through the years.

What exactly is it that we have lost? We've lost the recognition that spirit is the animating force in all life. All life, whatever form that life may take. There is real value to this belief because when all things are recognized for having spirit they become worthy of respect and consideration. We humans treat badly the things to which we assign little or no value.

St. Francis referred to the nonhuman kingdoms as "our little brothers." Joseph Campbell called them, "the little fellows."

A question looms large: Must we have dominion, or ruling power over other life forms to maintain our own worth? Do we think that to value others reduces our own stature? Do we become less? The concept of "protector" would substitute nicely.

St. Francis referred to the nonhuman kingdoms as "our little brothers." Joseph Campbell called them, "the little fellows." Must we have dominion over others to maintain our worth? Do we think that to value others reduces our own stature? Do we become less?

Well, of course, there are still some who deny that we even have a spirit. To them I respectfully whisper: Stay your judgment awhile. But don't wait too long out there in the dark and soulless cold. Come in and warm yourselves by the cheering hearth-fire of good fellowship in the kinship with all life.

It might be said that the loss of animism is the loss of unity with all life. Lacking connection we become mistrustful and coldly estranged, cut off from the great scheme of things. The philosopher, Martin Buber might likely say that estrangement exists in an "I-It" world rather than a reverential "I-Thou" world engaged in a conversational relationship with the Creator.

Denying or forgetting to acknowledge the unique functions of all "life streams," our lives become less complete, less satisfying, less interesting, less joyful, and, well, less entertaining.

Isn't it time to recognize all of these complimentary life streams for the unique functions they perform? Isn't this worth our consideration for the sake of our Earth?

"Reverence for all life," is the way Dr. Albert Schweitzer put it.

May the great circle be completed: from animism to polytheism, to the high God above, and finally, to the God in All-That-Is.

And one far-off divine event to which the whole of creation moves."

Alfred Lord Tennyson,
"In Memorium A. H. H.," 1850

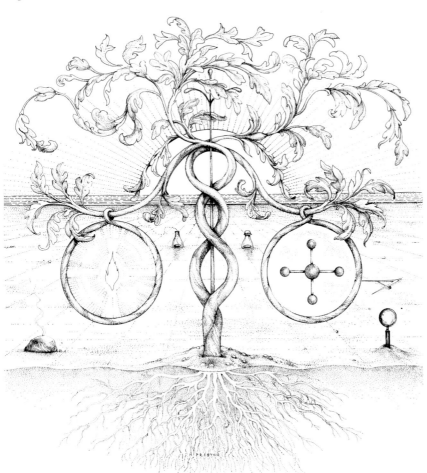

Plant Your Own Sacred Grove

If sacred groves were so useful in connecting people with the infinite, why not consider planting our own for the same purpose? These days, the closest we get to the old sacred groves are forests, parks, and, maybe, botanical gardens. While we're delighted to have these retreats from the frantic demands of everyday life, they're not exactly private and it's a rare soul who thinks of them as sacred. Of course the ancient groves weren't exactly private either, but everybody *knew* they were sacred.

Though we picnic in parks among trees, we've lost the concept of forests as natural holy places. Our kinship with Nature was lost when we forgot that we too are part of nature. Some city kids have so little exposure to nature that they actually fear it.

If we take the position of regarding Nature as a partner, we might update the idea a little to keep sacred groves in our lives, if only as quiet places to examine our thoughts.

The Idea

The idea is appealing. It would be good to have a personal meeting place between nature and us. Nothing grand—we can do without a high priest, vestal virgins, and a sacred fire. We just want a little sacred grove away from everyday life. But the yard is treeless, and our favorite park bench by the big tree probably is occupied, and the nearest woods are far away.

As we imagine the mysterious sacred groves of long ago, an idea begins to percolate. Why not make our own sacred grove? We fondly remember back to the tree house of our childhood, a retreat of our own, arranged exactly to our own specifications. Who needs a whole forest anyway? As the idea begins taking on speed we recapture the joy of youthful anticipation in creative adventure.

We could design a grove in that small plot of earth over there. How many trees to make a grove? If the trees are arranged in a triangle, three trees would make a perfectly adequate "grove." The space beneath and between them would become a sort of "room." Each tree trunk would be as a corner, like a "post," and the branches would become the "roof." We like this idea.

So we plot out a triangle of maybe 6 feet or 8 feet to a side. Here, we will plant a tree in each of its three corners.

We'll need to choose trees that are suited to our location, suitable for sitting under, suited to our personality, and also suitable to our size, now and eventual. We imagine ourselves sometimes lying there, gazing up into the boughs swaying above, stretched out upon the sacred soil of our grove, within the triangle of our trees. There the gods will smile upon us.

A rational thought interrupts: "This is going to take time and involve sweat, and didn't we have an appointment or . . . " Then a surge of irrepressible joy bubbles up as we again warm to the vision and dream on, thinking, "This much fun is definitely worth a little sweat." Besides, with some planning we could create a grove in a day (two, if the phone rings, three if it rains . . .)

"Mind is the builder," as Edgar Cayce, the famous American psychic, said. It all starts with an idea. The greatest cathedral started in the mind of its architect.

We are landscape architects with a plan. "We shall plant birches."

Progress Report

Three splendid, 8-foot birch trees are purchased from Sunnyside Nursery. Their trunks are smooth and papery-white with here and there little brown flecks, dark bracelets and chevrons that are their typical markings. We happily anticipate the frilly, heart-shaped leaves that will turn from summer green to spectacular golden-yellow, spangling against an autumn sky; and in winter, small brown catkins will gracefully drip from the dark, delicate branches. (Bonus: We are pleased to read that birches have an antibiotic effect on soil.)

The trees are waiting in their burlap wrappings and will be delivered tomorrow. They will suit our personality since a liking for change is well satisfied by the seasonally transforming birch. (If there happens to be a mystic strain of Druid in your blood, choose oaks.)

The right spot for our grove was chosen; it's a relatively away place, for privacy. If there were not a suitable away place, we would devise suitable camouflage, erect an invisible barrier, install a charming fence or some protective device.

Procedure

Preparing the earth is easier than expected. The earth is raked level. Then the perfect locations for the trees are marked on the ground with a handful of white baking flour (easily erased). The points of the triangle are equal distances apart (our choice.) Three holes are dug a little larger and a little deeper than the trees' root-balls. The nursery guy said to add planting-mix to the soil so the roots will grow easily. We plant them just a little above ground level, being careful to bury only the root-ball and not the trunk. We water them well, then deeply, once a week. After about a year they won't require much water at all.

We have created a grove, an instant "place." (Well, almost instant, since we did get involved in a phone call.) We are elated.

Now we will make a sacred space of our place. We might create a small ceremony, dedicating and blessing each tree, pronouncing each of them sacred, promising to protect them.

We will use lofty thoughts to dedicate them: Peace, Joy, Love, Harmony, that sort of thing. We choose thoughts that we want to bask in. We invent a simple phrase: 'Peace, joy, and harmony are with me always, glowing and growing in this sacred place and in my heart.' Over time, as we repeat this little ritual, the essence of its meaning will settle in, available to nurture us whenever we visit our grove.

We remember reading that these sorts of thoughts set up a vibratory resonance that will eventually become part of our very life expression. We become what our minds habitually dwell on.

Now that we have three new tree friends, we might tell them our dreams, our troubles, and our heart's desires, for secrets are safe with trees, and we will enter our sacred grove with an attitude of anticipation.

We might even tuck a small personal treasure somewhere within this sanctuary of trees, a beautiful stone or a written message of our intentions sealed in a small jar to make it our own.

We will hold our grove apart from the outside world to protect its sanctity and to keep the rabble without (rabbits excepted.) Eventually we may encircle it with low shrubs for privacy, and plant some flowers.

Years Pass

The trees grew fast, more than twice our height now. Imagination guided us over the years as we celebrated special occasions there. We set up a tent one autumn and hung a small, round mirror from a branch to represent the moon (mirrors are sacred objects to the nature-loving Shinto of Japan.) The red streamers we tied are still fluttering from a few branches. And we played our guitar music because we heard that trees love and resonate to music.

It was wonderful communing with and feeling the spirit of all life, humming in our own holy place. We could actually feel the friendship of those trees. One of the best ideas we ever had: our own sacred grove.

After Words

- My friend Richard Carter calls his place, within the 3,500 redwood trees that he personally planted: "the Playpen."

- No land for a grove? Bring flowers in to grace your dwelling place. No home? Bless you, pick up a leaf to carry with you.

- Back when I lived in Glencoe, Illinois, a freak tornado roared like a freight train through our front grounds, ripping out two huge, handsome spruce trees. After mourning their loss, we decided to replace the missing trees with a natural indigenous woods. What a satisfying experience that was. It became my first sacred grove.

Conclusion

_____

The enchanted forest path we have been following has taken strange twists and surprising turns, just as life does. The stories chosen to be included are but a few of the many that still cram my files. I'd like to have told you the story about . . . but another time, perhaps.

My intention was to shine a light into some little-known areas of the forest, presenting a different, richer view than the dim one many of us have come to believe is the only one. May we evermore see trees and all nature with kinder, wiser eyes. And may these stories serve as a touchstone whenever you, too, encounter anything of an unusual nature. May this collection provide a base from which to explore your own sylvan path.

Tread lightly: The trees will thank you.

Choices

Pomegranate, Pecan, Pear, and Palm
Basswood, Baobab, Blackthorn, Balm
Persimmon, Pignut, Pawpaw, Pine
Laurel, Leatherwood, Lilac, Lime
Mimosa, Maple, Mango, May
Butternut, Bitternut, Buckeye, Bay
Osage, Orange, Olive, Oak
Kumquat, Kingnut, Knicker Karote
Nectarine, Nutmeg, Nemu, Nettle
Pick a tree on which to settle

Stuart Kenter

Bibliography

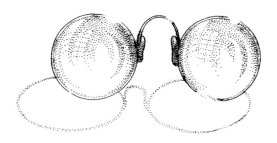

Abrahamsen, Aron, with Doris Abrahamsen and Don Margary. *On Wings of Spirit: A life Guided to Discover Spiritual Gifts.* Virginia Beach, VA: A.R.E. Press, 1993.

Abram, David. *The Spell of the Sensuous: Perception and Language in a More-Than-Human World.* New York: Pantheon Books, 1996.

Alpert, Richard [Ram Dass]. *Be Here Now,* San Cristobal, NM: Lama Foundation, 1971.

——*Grist for the Mill.* New York: Bantam, 1977.

Arno, Stephen. *Discovering Sierra Trees.* Yosemite Association and Sequoia Natural History Association in cooperation with the National Park Service, 1973.

Bagnell, Oscar. *The Origin and Properties of the Human Aura.* New York: University Books, 1970.

Backster, Cleve."Evidence of Primary Perception in Plant Life."*Journal of Parapsychology,* December.1967.

——*Primary Perception: Biocommunication with Plants, Living Foods, and Human Cells.* Edited by Franci Prowse. Anza, CA: White Rose Millennium Press, 2003.

Beckwith, Martha. *Hawaiian Mythology.* Honolulu: University of Hawaii, 1976.

Bendit, Phoebe D. *The Sacred Flame: A Study in Human and Devic Consciousness.* Wheaton, IL: Theosophical Press, 1962.

Berg, Yehuda. *The Power of Kabbalah: Technology for the Soul.* San Diego: Jodere Group, 2001.

Besant, Annie and C. W. Leadbeater. *Thought-Forms.* Wheaton, IL: Theosophical Publishing House, 1969.

Boone, J. Allen. *Kinship with All Life.* New York: Harper Row, 1976.

Bouchardon, Patricia. *The Healing Energies of Trees.* North Clarendon, VT: Journey Editions, 1999.

Boyer, Marie-France. *Tree-Talk: Memories, Myths and Timeless Customs.* London, New York: Thames & Hudson, Ltd., 1996.

Brennan, Barbara Ann. *Light Emerging: The Journey of Personal Healing.* New York: Bantam, 1993.

Burleigh, Robert. *Chocolate: Riches from the Rainforest.* New York: Harry N. Abrams, in association with the Field Museum, Chicago, 2002.

Burnham, Sophy. *A Book of Angels: Reflections on Angels Past & Present, and True Stories of How They Touch Our Lives.* New York: Ballantine Books, 1990.

Callahan, Kathy L. Phd. *Multisensory Human.* Virginia Beach, VA: A. R. E. Press, 1996.

Cayce, Edgar. *Auras: An Essay on the Meaning of Colors.* Virginia Beach, VA: A.R.E. Press, 1969.

Cerminara, Gina. *Many Lives, Many Loves.* New York: William Sloane, 1963.

Coe, Sophie D. and Michael D. Coe. *The True History of Chocolate.* New York: Thames & Hudson, 1996.

Cook, Roger. *The Tree of Life: Image for the Cosmos (Art and Imagination).* New York: Thames & Hudson, 1988.

Cowan, Elliot. *Plant Spirit Medicine.* New York: Swan-Raven, 1995.

David-Neel, Alexandra and Lama Yongden. *The Secret Oral Teachings in Tibetan Buddhist Sects.* San Francisco: City Lights Books, 1967.

Drummond, Richard Henry, PhD. *A Broader Vision: Perspectives on The Buddha and the Christ.* Virginia Beach, VA: A.R.E. Press, 1995.

Eberling, Ashlea. "Trees with Souls." *Forbes,* October 5, 1998.

Eisler, Riane. *The Chalice and the Blade.* New York: Harper & Row, 1987.

Emerson, Ralph Waldo. *The Complete Works of Ralph Waldo Emerson.* Centenary Edition. 12 vols. Cambridge, MA: Riverside Press, 1904.

Estes, Clarissa Pinkola, PhD. *The Faithful Gardener: A Wise Tale about That Which Can Never Die.* New York: Harper One, 1995.

The Findhorn Community. *The Findhorn Garden.* New York: Harper & Row, 1975.

Flint, Wendell D. *To Find the Biggest Tree.* Three Rivers, CA: Sequoia Natural History Association, 1987.

Fortune, Dion. *The Mystical Qabalah.* London: Earnest Benn, 1972.

Frankl, Viktor. *Man's Search for Meaning.* Boston: Beacon Press, 2000.

Frazer, James G. *The Golden Bough: A Study in Comparative Religion.* Gramercy Books 1993. (Orig. pub. 1890 in 2 vols., 1890.)

Fraser, J. Scott and Andrew D. Solevey. *Second-Order Change in Psychotherapy:*

The Goldern Thread That Unites Effective Treatments. Washington, D.C.: American Psychological Association, 2006.

Gallagher, Timmy. *The Gardens at Filoli.* Rohnert Park, CA: Pomegranate Artbooks, 1994.

Giono, Jean. *The Man Who Planted Trees.* Chelsea, VT: Chelsea Green, 1985.

Goodall, Jane and the National Geographic Society. *My Friends the Wild Chimpanzees.* Washington, D.C.: National Geographic Society, 1967.

Hafiz. *The Gift.* Translations by Daniel Ladinsky. New York: Penguin Group, (USA), 1999.

Hall, Manly P. *The Secret Teachings of All Ages.* 18th ed. Los Angeles: Philosophical Research Society, 1972.

Harner, Michael, PhD. *The Way of the Shaman: A Guide to Power and Healing.* New York: Harper & Row, 1990.

Hartzell, Hall and Jerry Rust. *The Yew Tree: A Thousand Whispers, Biography of a Species.* Eugene, OR: Hulogosi Communications, 1991.

Hovhaness, Alan. "The Ancient Tree." From a suite entitled *Spirit Murmur.* Shanghai String Quartet. Delos International, 1994.

Ishimoto, Tatsuo. *The Art of the Japanese Garden.* New York: Crown Publishers, 1968.

Itoh, Teiji. T*raditional Domestic Architecture of Japan.* Heibonsha Survey of Japanese Art, vol.21, translated by Richard L. Gage. Chicago: Art Media Resources, 1972.

Iyer, Pico. *Video Night In Kathmandu.* New York: Vintage Books, 1989.

Kaza, Stephanie. *The Attentive Heart: Conversations with Trees.* New York: Ballantine Books, 1993.

Jung, Carl G., M.-L. von Franz, Joseph L. Hendersen, Jolande Jacobi, and Aniela Jaffe. *Man and His Symbols.* Garden City, NY: Doubleday, 1964.

Lamott, Anne. *Bird by Bird: Some Instructions on Writing and Life.* New York: Anchor Books, 1995.

Lao Tsu. *Tao Te Ching.* Translated with introduction by D. O. Lau. New York: Penguin, 1963.

—— *Tao te Ching.* edited by Gia-Fu Feng and translated by Jane English. New York: Vintage Books, 1972.

Leadbeater, C. W. *Man Visible and Invisible.* Rev. ed. Wheaton, IL: Theosophical Publishing House, 1969.

Lessa, William A. and Evan Z. Vogt. *Reader in Comparative Religion: An Anthropological Approach.* Evanston, IL: Row, Peterson, 1958.

Lilly, John C. *Man and Dolphin.* London: Victor Vallance, 1962.

——*The Mind of the Dolphin: A Nonhuman Intelligence.* New York: Doubleday, 1967.

Lord, Albert. *The Singer of Tales.* 2nd ed. Edited by Stephen Mitchell and
Gregory Nagy, Cambridge, MA: Harvard University Press, 2000.

Lovelock, James. Letters to the editor: "Gaia As Seen through the Atmosphere."
Atmospheric Environment 6. 579–80 (1972): 579–580.

——"The Evolving Gaia Theory." Paper presented, UN University Lectures #1,
Tokyo, 1992.

Mason, Herbert. *A Verse Narrative: Gilgamesh.* New York: Mentor, 1972.

Maslow, Abraham H. "A Theory of Human Motivation." *Psychological Review 50*
(1943): 370–396.

Moore, Thomas. *Care of the Soul, A Guide to Cultivating Depth and Sacredness in
Everyday Life.* New York: HarperCollins, 1994.

Morse, Edward S. *Japanese Homes and Their Surroundings.* Rutland, VT: Charles
E. Tuttle, 1972.

Myss, Caroline, PhD. *Anatomy of the Spirit: The Seven Stages of Power and
Healing.* New York: Harmony Books, 1996.

Newhouse, Flower. *The Kingdom of the Shining Ones.* Escondido, CA: Christward
Publications, 1955.

Pert, Candace B., PhD. *Molecules of Emotion: Why You Feel the Way You Feel.* New
York: Simon & Schuster, 1997.

Preston v. State Board of Equalization, 4th series, vol. 25, Supreme Court of the
state of California (2001).

Renault, Mary. *The King Must Die.* New York: Vintage Books, 1958.

Rhoades, Michael. *Talking with Nature.* Tiburon, CA: H. J. Kramer, 1987.

Rifkin, Jeremy. *The Hydrogen Economy.* New York: Tarcher, 2003.

Robert, Hervé. *Les vertus thérapeutiques du chocolat.* Paris: Editions Artulen, 1990.

Schwarz, Jack. "Voluntary Control of Inner States of Consciousness II."
University of San Francisco Medical Center. Course given 1974.

——*I Know from My Heart.* Berkeley, CA: Celestial Arts, 1992.

Sheldrake, Rupert. *A New Science of Life: The Hypothesis of Morphic Resonance.*
Rochester, VT: Park Street Press, 1995.

Shelley, Percy Bysshe. "Ozymandias." Examiner, 1818.

Slesnick, Irwin L., et al. *Biology.* Glenview, IL: Scott, Foresman, 1980.

Spence, Lewis. The Mysteries of Britain: Secret Rites and Traditions of Ancient
Britain. London: Senate Studio Editions, 1994.

Steiner, Rudolf. Results of Spiritual Investigation. Blauvelt, NY: Rudolf Steiner
Publications, 1971.

Stone, Merlin. *When God Was a Woman.* Orlando, FL: Harcourt Brace, 1976.

Sugrue, Thomas. *There Is a River: The Story of Edgar Cayce.* Virginia Beach, VA:
A.R.E. Press, 1997.

Tennyson, Alfred, Lord. "In Memorium A H H." The Tennyson Page. http://charon.sfsu.edu/TENNYSON/tennyson.html.

Tomkins, Peter and Christopher Bird. The Secret Life of Plants. New York: Harper and Row. 1973.

Toms, Michael, and Justine Willis Toms. *True Work: Doing What You Love and Loving What You Do.* New York: Harmony/ Bell Tower, 1999.

Turnbull, Colin M. *The Forest People.* New York: Simon & Schuster, 1961.

Tylor, Edward Burnett. *Primitive Culture.* London: John Murray, 1871.

Watanabe, Yasutada. *Shinto Art: Ise and Izumo Shrines. Heibonsha Survey of Japanese Art.* Tokyo: Weatherhill/Heibonsha, 1974.

Western Garden Book. Menlo Park, CA: Sunset Books, 1997.

White, John, and Stanley Krippner. *Future Science, Life Energies and the Physics of Paranormal Phenomena.* New York: Anchor Books, 1977.

Wright, Machaelle Small. *Behaving As If the God in All Life Mattered.* Jeffersonton, VA: Perelandra Center for Nature Research, 1997.

Young, Ella. "Treets and Mountains." Interview on Pacifica Radio by Wallace Hamilton. Los Angeles: Pacifica Radio Archives #BB1036, 1960.

Zimmer, Heinrich. *Philosophies of India.* Edited by Joseph Campbell for Bollingen Foundation. Princeton, NJ: Princeton University Press, 1951.

Index

Index

My heartfelt gratitude to all those who have added to this book in so many different ways:

To my loyal and encouraging mother, whose spirit still lingers near, thanks for believing in me.

To my ever helpful and fun-loving husband, Alan, whose champion strength, enduring patience, and loving support have sustained me through the endless days and late nights working away in my studio, I can't thank you enough, and promise more carefree time.

To my wonderful, always dependable, sister Bonnie Rose Preston, for her skill, acuity, willing heart, selflessness, and valued assistance, I am truly thankful and fortunate.

To my great friend and colleague, Janet Alleyn, Production Manager/Designer extraordinaire, whose clear intelligence, elegant sensibilities, amazing expertise, whose depth of perception, and direction have been indispensable; without her guidance, this book could not have come into existence.

To my kind and scrupulous editor, Judith Chaffin, and to careful readers, John Collins, John Thomas, and Kari Popovic, for their keen, judicious evaluations, and sharp pencils, my deep appreciation.

And to my friends and family for their encouragement, suggestions and prayers:

Bea Agins, Shelly Arrowsmith, Dorothy Aksamitt, Esther Baran, Ellen Blonder, Nick Blonder, Cara Brown, Kathy Callahan, Richard Carter, Steve Coleman, Sally Cowan, Nancy Day, Nancy Doolittle, Ann Fox, Beth Fraser, Scott Fraser, Ingrid Gallagher, Norman Gilroy, Pat Grogan, Pam Hakman, Connie Hlavac, Elinor Hopcia, Gay Kagy, Stuart Kenter, Steve Kimball, Bruce Kortebein, Geraldine Lanier, Pamela Smith Leigh, Peter Leigh, Mea McNeal, Jessel Miller, Genna Panzarella, Judith Peck, Ross and Tom Perry (of Sunnyside Nursery), Joan Weinger Pressman, Bonnie Preston, Francis Rath, Marty Rice, Diane Richard, Judith Rothman, Ivan Saint John, Greg Schelkun, Priscilla Schelkun, Dorothy Slate, Mimi Tellis, Sanna Thomas, Dan Tomasek, Kris Trexler, and Renee Wahler, Lib Wilkinson.

Grateful Thanks to the following for permission to quote:

Cleve Backster, author of: *Primary Perception: Biocommunication with plants, living foods and human cells* (2003). White Rose Millennium Press. Franci Prowse, ed.

"Oaks, Rock Divas and a Tree Goddess" © 6/13/2008 by Justine Willis Toms and Michael Toms, co-founders of New Dimensions World Radio Broadcasting Network/Media and authors of *True Work: Doing What You Love and Loving What You Do.* wwwnewdimensions.org.

Excerpts from *Plant Spirit Medicine* by Eliot Cowan. Published by Swan Raven & Co. an imprint of Granite Publishing LLC.

Bea Agins, Cultural Anthropologist, graciously allowed me to tell her story which continues to unfold, bringing thoughtful change to her Ashual friend's tribe in the Amazon.

The Forest People by Colin M. Turnbull. New York.: Touchstone, an imprint of Simon & Schuster, Inc., 1961. Approximately 693 words (quotes from pp 60,74,91,159,248,272).

Behaving As If The God In All Life Mattered by Machaelle Small Wright. 3rd Edition. Published by Perelandra, Ltd., P.O. Box 3603, Warrenton VA 20188.

"Choices" verse used with permission. © 2008 by Stuart Kenter. Stuart Allen Books.

Design: Heather Preston
Art Direction: Heather Preston
Composition and Production Services: Janet Bollow Associates
Copy Editing: Judith Chaffin, Editorial Services
Scanning: Light Rain, San Rafael, California
Printer: Tien Wah Press

Printed and bound in Singapore

First Edition
10 9 8 7 6 5 4 3 2 1

Library of Congress Control Number: 2009900546

ISBN 13: 978-0-692-00111-0

Sweet Olive Press
Post Office Box 872
San Anselmo, California
94979

www.HeatherPrestonArt.com